THE WAY OF THE SATISFIED WOMAN

Also by Alanna Kaivalya, PhD

Myths of the Asanas:
The Stories at the Heart of the Yoga Tradition

Sacred Sound:
Discovering the Myth and Meaning of Mantra and Kirtan

Yoga Beyond the Mat: How to Make Yoga Your Spiritual Practice

THE WAY OF THE SATISFIED WOMAN

Reclaiming Feminine Power

ALANNA KAIVALYA, PhD

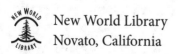

New World Library
Novato, California

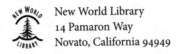

New World Library
14 Pamaron Way
Novato, California 94949

Text design by Tona Pearce Myers

Library of Congress Cataloging-in-Publication Data

Names: Kaivalya, Alanna, author.
Title: The way of the satisfied woman : reclaiming feminine power / Alanna Kaivalya, PhD.
Description: Novato, California : New World Library, [2024] | Includes bibliographical references. | Summary: "Mythology expert Alanna Kaivalya presents a new paradigm that defines the feminine journey for the modern age, empowering women to transcend masculine conceptions of success and flourish on their own terms"-- Provided by publisher.
Identifiers: LCCN 2024031656 (print) | LCCN 2024031657 (ebook) |
    ISBN 9781608689385 (paperback) | ISBN 9781608689392 (epub)
Subjects: LCSH: Feminism. | Women.
Classification: LCC HQ1155 .K353 2024 (print) | LCC HQ1155 (ebook) |
    DDC 305.42--dc23/eng/20240716
LC record available at https://lccn.loc.gov/2024031656
LC ebook record available at https://lccn.loc.gov/2024031657

First printing, November 2024
ISBN 978-1-60868-938-5
Ebook ISBN 978-1-60868-939-2
Printed in Canada

10   9   8   7   6   5   4   3   2   1

*To my grandmother, a woman who endured a life
in which she was denied agency so that I could live
to be empowered with so much of it.*

Satisfaction is the *pleasure* derived from the fulfillment
of one's wishes or needs.

May all your needs be met and may all your wishes come true.
I wish you all the pleasure and satisfaction this life has to offer you
as you walk the way of the Satisfied Woman.

Contents

1

Redefining Femininity for the Satisfied Woman

What if there was a way to become a fully Satisfied Woman: one who measured meaning on her own terms, recovered her feminine power, dropped masculine expectations for herself, and ascended to her own queenly throne? What if you could have your needs, desires, and cravings fulfilled in a way that empowered, enlightened, and enlivened you? What if you could do this outside the constraints of the patriarchy and beyond the bounds of current cultural limitations?

This is the way of the Satisfied Woman.

Becoming the Satisfied Woman relies on a foundation of femininity — tried-and-true qualities that are ingrained into the fibers of our being and the tendrils of our soul — as well as a bold new integration of our femininity with modern ideals and unexplored possibilities. The Satisfied Woman is a healed woman, rectifying past patriarchal wrongs within herself and extending that new balance into the world she creates around her. She measures life, not through success, but through satisfaction — the pleasure she derives through the fulfillment of her wishes and needs.

For the last century, women have fought for equality. But have we been fighting the right battle on the right field? In the struggle to gain ground, we have lost the liberty to be fully feminine, because the measures of success, happiness, and freedom have been defined primarily by men. As a result, women have had their unique needs overlooked — and have overlooked these needs themselves. In the pursuit of this masculine paradigm, even the most "successful" women find themselves exhausted, overwhelmed, and often isolated from what makes them truly happy: deep connection to their feminine nature.

As women, we have grown up being asked to play small, be quiet, smile often, and look pretty. At the same time, we have also been encouraged to develop careers, fend for ourselves, and be more logical. The bar for success is measured by men, and so we chase after the same things they do, in the same ways that they do.

What if there was a different way?

We need to let go of the masculine definitions of *success* and instead redefine our goals as the pursuit of satisfaction. Success suggests an end point: a goal to be reached, which is a supremely masculine aim. For women, life is circular and cyclical and filled with change. We know that rather than an end goal, there is only the next cycle, the next phase, the next passion or creative pursuit. Rather than setting markers for success that lead to a nebulous finish line, let us set metrics of satisfaction.

Lest you think that satisfaction is some mediocre achievement, let me offer you a formal definition. Satisfaction is the pleasure derived from the fulfillment of one's wishes or needs.

Doesn't get much more deeply pleasing — *satisfying* — than that! By fulfilling our needs and wishes, we come into accord with what is most alive within us. We achieve more than success: we actually feel joy as a result of satisfaction. Success doesn't always end that way. In fact, many who achieve "success" only feel that they want more, or they feel empty upon the completion of the goal! Not to mention that success can be a very lonely pursuit.

Not satisfaction, though. Satisfaction is inherently accompanied by joy. And because of our human nature, that means those around us share those positive feelings, too. We cannot feel joy when those around us are experiencing pain, discomfort, sadness, anger, inequity, oppression — anything on the negative spectrum of emotion. Our human empathy makes it so that happiness is real only when shared.

This means that everyone benefits from a woman's satisfaction.

Most women are not even aware that their femininity has needs, desires, and cravings that differ wildly from those of their masculine counterparts, much less that getting those needs met results in satisfaction for her and those around her. In fact, much of what makes the feminine powerful has been vilified, repressed, estranged, demonized, and purposely overlooked. What strong, opinionated woman hasn't been called a "bitch" in the conference room? We all know women who are belittled for "not doing enough" for their family. And as women, no doubt at some point in our lives we have been labeled "crazy."

Not to mention, we are often shamed for the feminine qualities that would make us more powerful if we brought them forward confidently! For example, the inherent feminine capacity for collaboration and connection might drive a feminine woman to invite several others into a thoughtful discussion to figure out the best solution to an issue, one that benefits everyone involved. But when we engage in this kind of collective dialogue, it is seen as a weakness, an inability to make our own decisions, and a pandering to others. In contrast, the masculine might just brazenly take the reins and assume the lead, forgoing any teamwork in favor of making an executive decision. The masculine and the feminine *are just different*, and the ways of the feminine are certainly no less "correct" or valuable!

What we most desperately need is a redefinition not just of womanhood and femininity but of many of the concepts and qualities that coincide with the feminine and a generous structure within which to contain it. Because our current culture has most valued and emphasized the masculine and its pathways to success and ideals of happiness, we have lost a sense of pride around and ownership of the incredible qualities that empower and satisfy the feminine.

What if, through redefining and reclaiming femininity on the basis of its own values and ideas, we unleashed its true potential — and in the process actually achieved balance for both sides? The reality is that each of these fundamental energies, the masculine and the feminine, needs for the other to be expressed in the highest and healthiest way possible in order for everything to be in balance!

Many women today are nowhere near balance. Instead, we are being asked to do it all: pursue a successful career and be full-time parents, do the dirty work and be sexy and available, fend for ourselves entirely and be willing partners at the drop of a hat. Not only is this incredibly confusing, but it is overwhelming and exhausting. Women spend so much time occupying the masculine polarity that the way of the Satisfied Woman has been lost.

So much so that when I talk about the most powerful qualities of the feminine, many women (including me!) often negate, diminish, apologize for, or completely disown those qualities. For example, when I point out that the power of feminine intuition is the driving force behind positive disruption and change, women tell me they have lost access to their intuition, or they don't know if it's "right," or they repress it in favor of logic, or they listen to their masculine counterparts who dismiss their intuitive knowing out of hand. When I tell women that leaning into their emotions is a key component of being a Satisfied Woman, they share stories of how they were told they were pretty only when they smiled or that their emotions were too much for others around them to handle.

The feminine is so much more than it has been given credit for, and the qualities that have been shamed, stripped, oppressed, and vilified have been so because, when expressed in their highest forms, they are qualities that wield unbelievable power and effectively change the world. There is fear at the heart of feminine repression, fear that too much balanced feminine disempowers the masculine. Of course, for the distorted or imbalanced masculine, that is a very scary thought.

Powerful women are often silenced, disbelieved, or worse. Even today this continues to happen as reproductive rights are stripped away and women have to struggle for basic care.

It is time to do things differently. It is time to take back the power inherent in our femininity. It is time to walk the way of the Satisfied Woman.

We need to begin by undoing and redefining the terms and concepts that have been altered to make us suppress or overlook these essential parts of ourselves. Because we are members of this masculine-dominated culture, even the modern woman often denies the feminine qualities that society has deemed weak, unacceptable, and/or uncontrollable.

Let's start with the term itself: *feminine.* Most people assume the word relates to anything female, but what I want us to lean into here is the dynamic psychic (as in "of the psyche") energy that is opposite and complementary to the masculine. Every human, regardless of gender assigned at birth, has both masculine and feminine energy in their psyche. At various times in our life, we may express one more than another for different reasons. For example, the masculine polarity is great for starting projects and leading the charge, and the feminine polarity finds ways of managing the project so that everyone gets their ideas heard. Of course, any gender can do both of these activities with excellence, and every person is capable of bringing forth either of these energies at any time.

However, each of us as individuals has a primary polarity, one that we most easily express, one that feels most comfortable and correct within our bodies and psyches. While it is often true that a woman's primary polarity is the feminine and a man's primary polarity is the masculine, this is not always the case. There are women who more clearly express the masculine and men who more clearly express the feminine.

That said, for the purposes of this book, I speak to people whose gender assigned at birth is female and who primarily express the feminine polarity. This is not because other genders and expressions are not valid — of course they are! But this book seeks to reframe femininity for cisgender women and offer support in releasing the paradigms of masculinity that have repressed and oppressed us for far too long.

Because women in this culture need help. I know, because I am one. And I spent decades in the wrong polarity, exhausted and overwhelmed. Through developing an understanding of what it means to be the Satisfied Woman, we have the potential to reclaim our energy and lead more authentic lives that align with our greatest strengths, creating incredible satisfaction.

Along this journey, we need to get comfortable with ideas that have been previously defined as uncomfortable or unacceptable. Like, for example, the concept of receptivity. The feminine is a receptacle for life and life energy. She wields it and moves it through her body, and it is sensual and energizing for those around her, most potently so for those in intimate partnership with her. The ability to receive enables the woman to feel pleasure and, in turn, offer pleasure and delight.

However, in a cultural distortion of masculine and feminine, this receptivity is often taken advantage of when women are asked to take on more than necessary or more than feels pleasurable. It is further distorted when a woman is forced in any way to receive — to be penetrated by the masculine — whether it be conversationally, relationally, or sexually. The discomfort with feminine receiving centers around the real fear of being taken advantage of in all the ways that happens: being raped or stripped naked of the valuable joy and life force that are inherently feminine. This is a real fear! Receptivity cannot be performed if the environment is not safe, if fear is present or trust is lacking. But where trust, love, and safety exist, one of the most powerful acts of the feminine is to be receptive. And one of the most glorious expressions of the masculine is not penetration, but heartfelt generosity. When generosity is freely contributed by the masculine, everyone receives joy, pleasure, and life energy through the feminine.

I will explore the concept of receptivity (and healthy relationship) more deeply in later chapters. Here I just want to provide an example of how we need to rewire our bodies and psyches to withstand the positive energy of the feminine force that flows within us. As we have been enculturated in the masculine paradigm, we have lost the wisdom of the ways of the feminine, and we need proper training in order to embody it fully in a safe, healthy, and satisfied way in all areas (and ages!) of our lives: family, career, relationship, and personal growth. Consider this book your guide to reclaiming the uniquely feminine qualities that reveal your most authentic, relaxed, and empowered self. When we, as women, learn to lean into our feminine nature, we also embolden those around us to express their primary polarity in the healthiest way.

Of course, some people struggle with, are incapable of, or are even resistant to this expression. Our feminine intuition guides us in knowing the spaces and people who are of greatest support to our well-being. And remember, every one of us has both polarities; clearly understanding the elevated qualities of each allows us to recognize the circumstances when one or the other is most helpful. This book isn't about only expressing the feminine. Rather, it provides a structure and guide for embracing your inherent feminine polarity and allowing all the parts of you to shine at the right time in the best way. This is as much an "undoing" as it is an "in-doing."

We have not just decades but centuries of patriarchal concepts to question and consider. These are written into our own lives as women. This fact requires us to shift our perspective and invite miracles, like the kind that happen when powerful women collaborate. That type of collaboration is often seen as either weak or dangerous, and so women have been taught to isolate from and compete with one another. We stand leery of our peers, as we have been trained that resources are thin and our abundance relies on our ability to overachieve or do everything ourselves. We may be so indoctrinated into doing everything or being all things to all people that we assume that is the natural way of the feminine.

It is not. Instead, the feminine thrives when it has the ability to make choices that are in support of well-being. Luckily, one of the great qualities of the feminine is intuition. If we use it to listen to our internal signals, we discover when we are approaching exhaustion, doing too much, or trying to fit ourselves into other people's molds. But intuition has been squashed, like so many other precious feminine attributes, and we as women oftentimes second-guess our intuition in favor of the more masculine quality of logic.

We need to return to feeling. We need to return to ourselves. We need to stop giving ourselves away. When we do this, we regain our vitality and then are able to restore and feed not only our own creative juices but those of the people around us. Intuition is not scary, otherworldly, woo-woo, or even magic. It is built into our biology and gives us access to deep wisdom to make important instant decisions about our well-being. It is governed by the right side of the brain — the feminine, feeling side — and cutting ourselves off from it disables our ability to choose what is right for us.

If we can't choose what feels right, then we are often forced to choose what feels wrong, uncomfortable, unsafe, or inauthentic. It is time for us to honor and reconnect with one of the greatest gifts of the feminine: the deep intuitive knowing that has guided women throughout history to make the best decisions possible for our greatest well-being.

Later in the book, we will explore ways to do this in every area of our life. For now, I want you to get excited. I want you to feel and recognize that this power has been brewing in you all along. It has always been there — perhaps latent, perhaps misunderstood, perhaps repressed, perhaps feared, but it is there. Everyone has access to femininity, but for those of us women whose primary polarity is the feminine, accessing this fully unleashes a force that is waiting — no, *longing* to be expressed.

Let us find true equality, not on masculine terms, pursuing masculine goals, but on our own terms, underpinned by feminine values. Let's elevate the feminine and show those around us that our joy, success, and satisfaction benefit everyone. Let us begin to walk the way of the Satisfied Woman.

The Current Feminine Reality

Being a woman in the world is hard! It is taboo in this day and age to admit this — to admit that we might have any kind of weakness and that perhaps the world we live in isn't quite designed for us. But if truth be told, we struggle to thrive and find satisfaction in the current patriarchal paradigm.

As women, we are trained to uphold the standards set for us by masculine ideals *and to like it*. We're not meant to complain, or else we look weak. We definitely shouldn't try to off-load duties, or we look useless. Replaceable. And we absolutely should not express our valid needs, lest we be scolded for being too demanding.

This society and culture teach us from an early age to be quiet. Take it. Do more than what is asked of us. Succeed at all costs.

But what *has* this cost us?

Our femininity.

Our femininity is what makes us empowered, satisfied, and comfortable in our own skin. Our femininity serves our own needs as well as those of the people around us. And our femininity infuses life energy into the world, breeds creativity, and is the birthplace of imagination.

However, it is our femininity that is repressed, vilified, and condemned by modern culture. No doubt you have heard buzzwords like *the patriarchy* and *toxic masculinity* being tossed around as we enter a time of reckoning, reconciliation, and re-creation. We are questioning how the past few thousand years have gone and wondering how to make the next many years better for ourselves and the women who come after us.

This book is not about masculinity, the patriarchy, the toxicity of both, or the dismantling of either. However, it is nearly impossible to discuss the feminine and the state we find ourselves in today without talking about these things or how we got here. After all, we are trying to survive in a primarily patriarchal structure with the rules of masculinity dominating us. There has not been room for feminine structures or cycles, and the needs of the feminine have not been heard or understood for quite some time.

It is time.

Within the past hundred years, the world has been privileged to see women rise up and fight for their rightful, equitable place in the world. With the suffragettes of the early twentieth century, the women's rights movement of the 1960s and '70s, and the #MeToo movement of the early part of the twenty-first century, the struggles and suppression of women were finally being voiced, reevaluated, and revalued.

However, all these movements have taken place within a patriarchal culture, where even many of us women have a difficult time operating by anything other than patriarchal rules. It's no one's fault. The intention here isn't to place blame or pit one polarity against the other. In fact, just the opposite. When the qualities of a more balanced society are achieved, divisions dissolve, and symbiosis occurs. But it's not balanced to have women fighting on men's terms.

We need our own terms.

While we have a twenty-five-hundred-year (or more!) cultural legacy of patriarchy, before that, much of the world existed as matriarchal societies. Now, we have to bear in mind that this was prehistoric, and they also didn't have a lot of the tools and concepts we work with today, like reliable contraception, bills of rights, or the practices of modern medicine. People in prehistory also didn't have the language of psychology that we do today, which allows us to take a meta look at the mind and understand its complexity. These societies were more basically concerned with living to the ripe old age of thirty-five (the average lifespan), protecting the safety and well-being of the tribe, and advancing the human race through procreation.

Different times. Different problems.

One era is not better than the other, it's just that we're living in this one. Rather than idealize the matriarchal societies of thousands of years ago, what I find more interesting to do is to look at what worked (or didn't!) within them and what might help us *thrive* as women in our current reality today.

The challenge with either a matriarchal or patriarchal society is that each version values *power over* the other polarity. Even in matriarchal societies of old, women held power *over* men, made decisions *for* men, and *controlled* assets and resources. Because we know how this feels, we can easily see why the founders of the patriarchy we live in today fought so hard to gain power, control, and decision-making privileges!

If we are looking to achieve something new, something stronger, something more balanced, then we must seek to establish methods of influence that incorporate generosity and surrender, power that empowers everyone, and decisions that are made for the highest good of everyone involved. While this may sound like a Pollyanna ideal, we find some evidence of this having existed in matriarchal societies when we look to what they valued. What were they most concerned with having power, control, and decision-making abilities over?

The family and the tribe.

It wasn't about status, prestige, esteem, or personal glory. It was about making sure that the family unit or the tribe was *thriving*. Sometimes that did require difficult decision-making and strategizing, like when one tribe battled another over resources. Sometimes it did require some control, like when it came to an aberrant member causing harm to another. Sometimes it did create power differentials, because at the end of the day, a clear yes or no is necessary.

If both matriarchy and patriarchy equal hierarchy, what are we to do?

We lean fully into our essential feminine nature. Not in a way that abdicates power and allows anyone to have agency over any part of us, but in the same way that water flows around a rock. The rock may be immovable, but it is still moved, carved, and reshaped by the flowing, graceful power of water.

Think of masculinity as the rock: a solid, steady presence. And of femininity as the water: a graceful, flowing change.

It is the water that determines the course of the life-sustaining river, not the rocks.

Rather than focus on hierarchical structures that always leave someone powerless, let's set a vision for a future where it is through one another's strength that everyone is empowered. This requires us to remain steadfast in our feminine ideals, powerfully rooted in our intuitive and emotional guidance, and firm in our desire to commune and collaborate for the highest good of all. Without this, the life-giving waters of the feminine either freeze solid in a deranged faux-masculine state, or they evaporate completely, vaporizing away until rain brings us back to the earth.

This is a lofty vision. It is both an individual and a collective vision. I imagine empowerment in apartments, where people living in partnership find their water-over-rock ideals, as well as in the houses of government, where the collective finds balance through steadfastness *and* graceful change.

As you read this book, remember that this work starts within you. When you are able to achieve even a little more of this sacred balance within your own daily life, it has a ripple effect — just like the feminine waters — on those around you. And as more women read this book along with you (please, pass it along!), we move this life-giving and life-changing water from the streams to the rivers to the great, vast oceans.

This work starts inside of us. Just as all life does.

We are the Satisfied Women. We are the changemakers. We are the birthers of new life and of a new way of living.

Reality Check

I hope that all sounds inspiring and rings of truth to the depths of your soul. Trust me, the promise of an empowered world where all women find their own satisfaction is what propels me out of bed in the morning.

Here's my truth: Writing this book feels heavy. Loaded. It feels like the kind of book that needs to change the entire society it's written in.

I hope it does.

As I write this, I find myself in certain places apologizing for my assertions and recognizing that this is one of the most unbalanced manifestations of the repressed feminine.

We need to stop apologizing for ourselves.

Having grown up in this patriarchal society, I'm subject to its assertions, too. Assertions like: Women should play small and subservient (especially to men). The only way to succeed in life is on men's terms. Somehow women need to do it all and still maintain a level of sex appeal in the bedroom.

At every turn in this book, I find myself nearly writing an apology or a mitigation. Something like, "Women need to be safe, but oh it's so hard to create safety right now." Or like, "Women need to be cherished," and then I proceed to overexplain *cherishing* to try to make it OK for the reader.

Look, here's the truth.

Women need to be safe.

Women need to be cherished.

Full stop.

And why do we need to overexplain or apologize for those needs? To be safe, cherished, free to be our wild, intuitive selves, and loved for every inch of it is every woman's right.

While it is the unfairness of the ages that these rights are really difficult for every woman to come by, I certainly don't need to apologize for it. Neither do you.

We didn't create this culture or these paradigms. We just live in them.

It's way past time they change.

This is my sincere hope for this book: that it prompts positive change for the feminine.

I want it to change you. I want it to change me, too. And I really hope that those who buy into patriarchy read it and it changes them. Forever. Or at least gives them something to seriously consider. Because women are powerful. So powerful.

Not powerful like men.

Powerful like women.

Our power comes through our grace, our intuition, our collaboration, our receptivity, our ability to see all sides, our wild and authentic emotions.

Our power comes through our femininity.

When we bring it forth, it soothes us, heals us, downregulates our nervous systems, puts us into alignment with the highest expression of who we are, and enables us to fulfill our purpose. It does this for those around us, too.

The feminine is necessary. It is one half of a whole. It is the counterbalance to the masculine. It is the down to the up, the negative pole to the positive pole, the introspection to the extroversion, the Shakti to the Shiva, the yin to the yang.

Actually, if we consider the metaphor of the lovely yin-yang symbol, we see a perfect circle with complementary dark and light halves gracefully filling the inside. As a circle, it rolls on down the road of life perfectly well, its two pieces coexisting peacefully and each in support of the other.

Take one of those halves away, and you are left with a paisley shape: immobile on its own and unable to roll anywhere. Both the yin and the yang — the feminine and the masculine — are equally and opposingly necessary to complete the shape required for harmony.

Misshape one of those halves through distortion or imbalance, and we have a problem. The circle doesn't roll. One half gets squished or left behind. The other becomes inflated or overwhelming.

Each of these energies is complete in itself *and* incomplete without the other.

Remember the old saying "It takes two to tango"? Imagine those tango dancers before you now, each in their brilliant red and black outfits, moving seamlessly to the complicated rhythm of the music. The feminine partner is the follower, receiving her companion's lead almost intuitively as she stretches her leg backward, full of faith, to make every step. She glides across the floor, occasionally adding her own flourish of toe, knee, or glance, to bring mystery and vibrancy to the dance. She is mesmerizing on her own, and all eyes are on her. But without her partner, the dance is empty.

Her masculine partner provides strength and support as he holds his hand high on her back and, through the most subtle cues, provides direction and structure to their movement. While she adds the creativity and mystery and makes the dance tantalizing and her own, he offers the decisions required for the steps they will both take. His steady hand, his calming presence are the basis of the dance. Her poise, intuitive movement, and embodiment of delight are why we enjoy it.

The feminine runs joy and pleasure through her body in the dance. When she is in full receptivity, the dance looks flawless. The masculine holds her firmly in an embrace, providing safety and leadership, while she glides backward, completely trusting that her partner is leading her in the right direction.

Each partner is absolutely necessary. And when they fulfill their energetic roles well and in full alignment with their given polarity, the two of them become perfectly entangled — each whole and complete in and of themselves and yet completely entrained with the other.

I don't know if you've ever danced the tango, but it really is the perfect metaphor for this symbiotic energy. Nothing quite like ballroom dance requires humans to exist in opposite polarity to express themselves so fully.

If only we could do that in every aspect of our life.

I've spent years as a student of the Argentine tango. While I have studied and danced many different styles of ballroom technique, only Argentine tango truly lets me slide so fully into the feminine polarity. This specific style demands it.

Sometimes you can get away with a little strength and assertion in swing. You can exhibit a little rigidity in cha-cha. But Argentine tango forgives nothing when it comes to the feminine slipping out of her polarity. It's absolutely divine.

When I finally realized this in my dance lessons, I was absolutely hooked.

Funny thing was that I initiated dance lessons with my then-husband as a way for us to participate in something together. We simply weren't connecting, and I couldn't figure out why. As soon as we hit the dance floor, the issue became readily apparent. He had difficulty initiating the steps and making the decisions about where to move on the dance floor. And I couldn't stop trying to make decisions about where to move on the dance floor and taking steps of my own.

I was firmly stuck in the masculine polarity. He had abdicated his masculinity to me and settled into the feminine polarity. Not only was it uncomfortable, but it was unsatisfying and prompted further separation between us.

After years of living alone, running my own business, and being a teacher and educator, I was used to handling everything myself, executing plans, and driving the show for everyone around me in business, in intimate partnership, and even with friendships and family.

And I was completely exhausted.

Maybe this rings true for you, too.

Many modern women, in order to survive the current culture,

find themselves in situations where they have to "man up" or "grow some balls," where they have to "wear the pants" or "stop being a pussy."

My fellow feminine women, may I recommend that from here on out, *you own your pussy?*

As Traver Boehm, founder of the UNcivilized movement for men, would say: "The pussy is the portal."

I tend to agree.

Rather than cringe at any negative connotation of that word, I strongly suggest we take it back. After all, it is ours. And our pussy is the physical portal to pleasure and to life itself. We own that.

That is *powerful.*

It is also an energetic representation of all that is feminine. It is quite literally a receptacle, and women are receivers. Femininity embraces receptivity and empowers others through it. Our bodies and wombs follow the inherent cycles of nature, and whether we are connected to that or disconnected, our innate feminine intuition always pulls us back to it through the pussy when we bleed right on schedule (or gives us information about internal imbalances when we don't).

Our femininity, our pussy portals, our pleasure, our life-giving forces, our sacred emotions, and our intuitive guidance all create the most extraordinary potential for a life that is fully satisfied and joyous at every level. For those readers, like me, who have spent way too long either repressing their own femininity or trying to wear the mask of the masculine, I've got you. It's time to recalibrate, embrace your feminine essence, and *thrive.*

Part of thriving is knowing how and when to settle into your natural feminine polarity. If the life you have created has shifted you overwhelmingly and exhaustingly into the masculine paradigm, then any steps — even baby dancing steps — will be relief filled and life-affirming. Let me give you some steps here in this book. I hope you use them to express yourself as fully, femininely, and fluidly as possible.

2

Defining Polarities and Understanding the Satisfied Woman

The universe exists in polarities: light and dark, up and down, above and below, positive and negative, masculine and feminine. It is through these opposites that we find wholeness and balance. One cannot exist without the other, and yet each one in and of itself is a complete thing. It's possible to define light on its own, but we never understand it fully unless we know the dark. It is the same with the masculine and feminine energies that exist throughout nature and within every human psyche. Each is definable, essential, and independent, but incomplete without the other.

We all have access to both polarities, and each is necessary at various times in our lives. We activate the masculine within us when we are goal driven and logically oriented. We lean into the feminine when we experience the fullness of emotion and are intuitively inspired.

On a soul level, most of us know the differences between the primary polarities of the feminine and the masculine. We live these differences every day within ourselves and in our relationships to others. Even though we know the simplest definitions of these primary psychic (as in "of the psyche") energies within humans, we as individuals usually spend a lifetime trying to understand them within us and within each other. (Think of the great success of titles like *Men Are from Mars, Women Are from Venus*.) Whether we are attempting to strike the right balance of these energies within us or we are leaning into our primary polarity to strike that balance in relationship with another, all of us navigate these psychic polarities every day.

Even in our most basic biology, there is a difference — a separation — between masculine and feminine and how they may be expressed through gender and form. Whether we carry XX or XY chromosomes determines the expression of our physical bodies, attributes, growth, development, and aging process. Our DNA affects our brains, our attitudes, our habits, and our tendencies. In addition to this, the circumstances of our birth, our family, our culture, and all our childhood events, including traumas, contribute to the way our body and psyche develop and how we express these polarities. The body we are born in comes with both cultural expectations and certain physical attributes dictated by biology and chronology. Especially for women, there is a biological life cycle that is shaped by time, DNA, and circumstance and informs our psychic reality and expression.

This biological life cycle, unique to women and the bodies we are born in, is a major factor in the energetic qualities of the feminine psyche. The onset of puberty and our ability to gestate and support life foster our inherent creativity (not just procreativity!). The fact that we have pussies and wombs means that we are the receivers — the receptacles — of the life force, and we are the harbingers of joy and pleasure. Because our natural hormones and their rhythmic cycles correspond to a range of emotional depth and experiences, we have an intuitive sense of the world that comes from our soul, and it must be heeded for us to feel safe and secure.

These inbuilt qualities — designed by Mother Nature right down to the cellular level — make women and the feminine expression of the psyche unique, special, and singularly connected to the natural world in undeniable ways. We must attune to this psychic truth as women and bring forth the feminine within us, not just to feel more comfortable in our bodies, but to affirm our essential place in the world. It is through the feminine we find deeper connection to the world and others around us, while the masculine seeks to explore and conquer it. In their own way, each of these energies is valid, but we are at a time in history when that connection has been lost and conquering has become dangerously destructive. Nevertheless, the masculine and feminine energies within the psyche remain present, while separate. At odds, yet symbiotic. Different, yet equal. And equally valuable.

While both masculine and feminine energies exist within each of us, there is one energy that prevails as our primary polarity. Throughout the day, year, or decade, hopefully we find ourselves smoothly sliding between one or the other based on what life or circumstance needs. However, we become most fully ourselves when we are able to comfortably and confidently express our true nature by leaning into our primary polarity. As women, we are often misguided and uneducated in the possibilities of feminine potential. We have been taught to hide our glorious feminine attributes in favor of the masculine-dominated culture we live in.

For those of us in whom the primary polarity is the feminine, it is time to embrace and understand more fully what makes us women and to restructure and redefine the power, purpose, and ideals of women today. Let's create a fully satisfied life on our own terms. For too long, masculine paradigms have defined values in relationships, career, family, spirituality, and health. Think about what is expected of women in the home, or what society says an ideal woman looks like, or how she behaves in a relationship. Consider the bar for success and how our culture says women should achieve it.

Do you think those standards were set by women? Not a chance.

We live at an interesting time when women finally have the

agency and the visibility to choose differently. But how shall we do it? If we've only ever seen the values set forth by a patriarchal culture, how do we know what those values look like for the feminine?

We know by examining the essential nature of the feminine and translating that essence into satisfaction for ourselves. *This is the way of the Satisfied Woman.*

Defining the Feminine and the Masculine

Very simply put: The feminine is intuitive and emotionally based. The masculine is logical and thought driven. I know the reaction by many readers to even that simple definition is resistance. "Ugh! That's so reductive! Women are so much more than that! And sometimes even men aren't logical!"

Yes, this is all true. Humans are complex beings who are filled with both logic and emotion, no matter what gender. We need to better understand the fundamental essence of the dynamic psychic energies of the masculine and feminine polarities in every individual in order to differentiate accordingly. And what we further need to understand is our own primary polarity, so we can lean into that and honor it. This is how we fulfill the greatest privilege of our lifetime: to be completely ourselves.

As I've said, femininity is intuitive, emotionally based, and rooted in unconscious drives and pleasures. (The pop term is *subconscious*. I use the proper psychological terminology here.) Her realm is the underworld, the dreamlike space that is rich with imagination, creativity, and mystery. The feminine is wild, carefree, and without linear direction. She prefers to move in circles and cycles, never minding to retrace a step if more joy and magic can be found in doing so. Community is her communion, and she seeks to collaborate and ensure that, through dialogue and understanding, everyone's needs are met and their highest good is served. Her creativity comes from within her and becomes unleashed when she feels secure and trusts her environment.

She thrives in spaces where she is securely held — delicately supported — within the type of boundaries that make rivers out of oceans and provide safe haven. She longs to move her body to the dance of the drumbeat within her, unabashedly and without fear that her body will be ravaged. She prefers to be ravished, taken in the throes of pleasure, driven by sensual and sensational feelings that linger in her mind, heart, breath, and breast. She always wants more and is open and receptive to what is generously and kindly (consensually) given. The feminine is a deep well — a receptacle — for the full expression of emotion, pleasure, and desire. When she is completely cherished, that cherishing inspires boundless joy and pleasure.

Femininity in and of itself is whole...but it is not absolute. Even within the body of the fiercely feminine woman, the masculine energy is present to lead, direct, protect, and contribute when necessary. The Swiss psychologist Carl Jung labeled the masculine energy within the female psyche the *animus* and the feminine energy within the male psyche the *anima*. His contention was that each opposite energy needs to be tended to and taken into consideration. One way to address this is by understanding how to honor each part of ourselves while remaining in our primary polarity. This could mean balancing our intuitive knowing against some logic or pushing through to a deadline while making sure to give our creative needs an outlet along the way.

For those of us who exist more fully in the feminine polarity, we relish opportunities to release completely into the feminine and offer trust to worthy masculine counterparts who provide a stable presence, confident courage, steady connection, and loyal guardianship. This is the other means of tending to the animus: through external relationship to the masculine. Because humans do not exist in isolation, because we thrive in connection to each other, we have the opportunity to unleash our feminine qualities and strengths in the presence of the healthy masculine men around us — whether they be friends, lovers, colleagues, or family members.

What is healthy masculinity? It is that faculty of the psyche that is consciously driven by reason and thought and is always considering the surest, most linear path forward. Forging ahead is a strength of the masculine as it proudly plows through obstacles, sometimes unabashedly, to cut a pathway that was not previously present. The masculine is strong, in the way that courage trumps fear and protectorship prevails over meekness. The masculine sees smallness as an opportunity to grow and weakness as a reason to press on. Though the masculine loves order and achievement, it deeply desires freedom and finds it most in unscheduled time — time on his own, left to his own devices, to explore his own passions and pursuits.

This unscheduled, restorative time is necessary for the masculine, who always feels the pull to his beloved feminine. The nature of the feminine is always to want more and to want it now, and the responsive masculine always strives to provide in a way that falls, not under obligation, but rather under contribution. The masculine generously gives to the feminine with his whole heart because she offers him joy, delight, and pleasure in return. He is deeply devoted to her and chooses to lovingly worship at her altar every chance possible. That worship is a divine connection between masculine and feminine where strength is received.

This dynamic interaction between masculine and feminine plays out in relationships on the outside as well as in the relationship between these energies within our psyche. While it is possible to navigate this dynamic within us as individuals, it is difficult to balance in a culture that so overtly emphasizes masculine values. Especially in women of the feminine polarity, the masculine tends to — perhaps unsurprisingly — take over and dominate, even within ourselves. Not to mention, we are taught to repress our inner feminine because its qualities are perceived as less valuable.

To become the Satisfied Woman, we must learn to cherish our own inner feminine qualities, just as we wish to be cherished by the masculine in our external relationships. We need to place confidence in our intuitive knowing and center its guidance, even as we honor the logic of our own mind. To be fully satisfied, we must let our feminine energy prevail within us, as we seek external opportunities, relationships, and life choices that esteem our femininity.

Femininity at Its Best

Femininity has its own qualities, its own standards, and its own realm of satisfaction. While the feminine and masculine are counterparts to each other, they are complementary, not competitive. They enhance and build on each other when they are both in their healthiest and fullest expression. They bring forth life and exuberance rather than squash it, and they empower and enhance each other rather than detract and diffuse.

For too long, though, femininity has been defined by the masculine, as its counterpart or its opposite. And in that way, it has been seen as weak, less than, undesirable, taboo, toxic, and even dangerous. All things feminine have been given the pink wash of delicacy, frailty, and breakability, and they have always been understood *in relation to* the masculine.

No more.

They both have their own power, their own relevance, and their own gifts to the world.

However, the world rarely sees the fullest, brightest expression of these qualities. Over the past several millennia, as this particular patriarchal culture has developed, the feminine has been consumed, commodified, and contained all to within inches of its life. Because the unbridled and self-expressive feminine is wild and free, it feels dangerous and unpredictable to the untempered and unconfident masculine. What's worse is that the distorted masculine lacks the self-confidence to share power and so seeks control over others, especially the feminine. Not recognizing that true power comes from *empowerment*, the distorted masculine has adulterated the feminine to the extent that even women hardly recognize it.

We are taught that the greatest expression of the feminine is quietness and meekness. It is not; it is wild and untamed. We are encouraged to either defer to the masculine by becoming helplessly submissive or assume the masculine energy ourselves, which puts us out of alignment with our true needs and hopelessly burns us out. We are isolated from each other as we are taught to suppress the very real urge of the feminine to commune and collaborate, and instead we compete with other women. We all know these conditions, and we recognize them in the women who won't speak up for themselves and don't get their needs met, in the women who mistrust and judge their fellow females, and in those who speak so loudly their needs are misunderstood or undermined.

Women today have been so trained and enculturated by our current society that it's not even that we have forgotten what femininity is or lost touch with our femininity; it's that the road map to the feminine's full expression is so completely buried, we were most likely never given knowledge of it in the first place.

Not anymore.

The feminine is wildness and freedom. It is unabashedly emotional and unquestioningly intuitive. It is circular and cyclical. It harbors creativity as well as demolition and reconstruction. And it seeks cooperation, collaboration, and companionship. The feminine is also unapologetically inquisitive, questioning the status quo and never blindly accepting rigidity, dogma, or doctrine.

It's easy to see how these fundamental qualities might scare someone rooted in a concrete belief system or someone firmly holding on to a linear way of doing things. It makes sense why fierce inquiry would be quashed by someone who thinks they have all the answers. It's easy to understand why women are taught to be skeptical of one another as a means of isolation. And it follows that wildness and freedom would be tamed by those who wish to corral and control.

It is no surprise that we find ourselves in this place at this time. If there is one primary driver of the desire to control, quash, and concretize, it is fear. Fear of the wildness and freedom of the feminine prompts its fierce control and demonization. So much so that even for those of us whose natural polarity is the feminine, we feel fear in its expression.

It is time to be fearless.

We are lucky to live in a time when women have stronger agency, more resources, and greater options for how to live our lives and establish our place in the world. We can choose what kind of career to pursue (or whether to have one at all), we can decide whom to partner with (or whether to partner at all), and we can determine the structures of our family, our homes, our passions, and our pursuits.

Historically, these things were determined for us by culture, religion, family, circumstance, and the men in charge around us. We were forced to marry men we didn't choose. Education was withheld. Our options were limited by the status of the men in our family.

Of course, there are circumstances even today that force women into these precarious and unholy positions. There are women now who are subject to discrimination, inequity, abuse, intolerance, and worse.

Every woman today continues to suffer to some extent from the mere fact that she was born a woman. Restrictions are still placed on us by society. There are places we cannot walk freely at night. There are doors that will never open simply because of our gender.

Which is why we must take the advantages and opportunities available to us while remaining diligently committed to creating even more conditions for femininity to thrive to the greatest extent possible. Our entire existence in this modern era is full of choices that women before us never had.

This raises a very new and essential question: How do we know which choices fully satisfy us as women?

First and foremost, in order to foster the foundation of a life of feminine satisfaction, we need these Four Keys:

- **Safety:** to be ourselves and free from harm in body, mind, and heart
- **Security:** to know that our needs are being provided for
- **Trust:** in ourselves, our situation, and those around us
- **To be cherished:** to have our emotions and intuition honored by the masculine

Having these Four Keys present in our lives gives us the ease and confidence to flourish in our femininity. We are relaxed and able to move pleasure through our bodies, embrace wild feminine creativity, and tap into our intuitive guidance to move forward on the path that is most authentically ours.

When these keys are not present, it is more than likely we will either slip into the masculine polarity to try to provide them for ourselves, burning ourselves out in the process, or else we will suffer from a distortion of the feminine, resulting in our needs and desires being misunderstood and unmet by those around us.

To the greatest extent possible, we need to bring these qualities into our lives by constantly making intuitive choices that allow more of them to be present and dismissing anything that detracts from them. This includes a heavy curation of our time, energy, pursuits, people, and interests. It's time to get fierce around keeping what feeds our feminine and releasing what does not. Once we recognize the empowerment and freedom that are possible when these Four Keys are present in our lives and the foundation of support they provide us as women, we need to establish them to the best of our ability and never look back.

Because it is possible to lead a life as the Satisfied Woman. On your own terms.

Who Is the Satisfied Woman?

While it sounds great that we should have the Four Keys firmly in hand and feel fully supported on our feminine journey, what does that actually mean? What does it look like to live life as the Satisfied Woman?

While there isn't one cookie-cutter representation of what the Satisfied Woman looks like, we know her because of her ability to embody and express the greatest attributes of femininity with confidence, wildness, and freedom. It doesn't matter if she's changing the motor oil or baking cookies: what qualifies as feminine isn't a list of activities assigned to gender, but rather the *way* any activity is undertaken. The feminine psyche looks for opportunities to collaborate, be creative, express beauty and sensuality, and enhance pleasure. These can all be achieved under any circumstance by the Satisfied Woman.

The Satisfied Woman is one embodying her femininity fully, leaning into her natural polarity, asking the world to revere her womanhood, and claiming her rightful place anywhere she desires to be.

She is the lady who is deeply comfortable with herself and her surroundings because she is:

- completely supported and free to be her wild, feminine self.
- tapped into her creativity and channels it regularly.
- sexually satisfied and able to run pleasure through her body.
- honoring her emotions and intuition as her primary decision-making forces.

This can be you, Satisfied Woman.

Imagine a life where you are intrinsically happy, surrounded by people who love and care for you, and you are utterly confident in that love and care. As the Satisfied Woman you are free to be yourself, because you are comfortable in your surroundings as well as who you are surrounded by. You are not afraid to feel and show emotion — it's completely safe for you to do so — because you are both *heard and believed.*

The Satisfied Woman is supported by and thrives on collaboration, connection, and the sharing of ideas. She surrounds herself with people who value her insights and wisdom, who are inspired by her gifts. She is receptive to their ideas and guidance and trusts fully that all outcomes serve the highest good. She is nourished by her female relationships; being with other women fosters creativity and growth and leads to new insights about her own and her friends' well-being.

A Brief Description of the Masculine

While this book is dedicated to femininity and the feminine woman, it is also helpful to understand what the healthiest expression of the masculine looks like, because we do not exist in isolation, and the feminine actually *thrives* in balance and harmony with the masculine. Even though the patriarchy is problematic and prompts distortion of both masculine and feminine energies, we must know the positive power and potential of the masculine so that we may seek it out in our intimate partners, allies, family members, friends, and colleagues.

We already know that the most fundamental energy of the masculine is logic based and goal driven, but the masculine is much richer and more textured than it is often given credit for. The best masculine men have big, big hearts filled with the courage to walk through fire to protect loved ones and do the right thing. They're purpose driven, and often their purpose is prompted by their commitment to being a provider: their ability to create a solid foundation and stability for those they love. They derive great joy and delight from being generous, especially toward the feminine. They are leaders and love making confident decisions that they know are in the highest interests of those around them. They value integrity and strive to make their actions match their words and ideals.

They also crave freedom — but in a different way than the feminine. While the feminine usually finds freedom through her creative expression (which feels wild to the masculine), the masculine finds freedom in unscheduled time (which feels unpredictable to the feminine). During unscheduled time, when no external demands or expectations are placed on him, the masculine is most energized and enhanced through passionate pursuits like sports, tinkering, adventure, or thrill seeking. Ladies, you know what I'm talking about if you've ever stumbled into a man cave during halftime or driven by a campsite filled with male best friends.

When the masculine feels controlled or senses an absence of freedom, rather than be energized by unscheduled time, his behavior distorts into procrastination — putting important things off for far too long because the notion of time itself feels like another constraint. Clearly, no one benefits from procrastination, and it increases pressure on everyone. Optimally, the masculine leans into free time as a respite from the pressures of life and uses it to reenergize himself into pursuing his passions and following the needs and desires of his courageous heart.

The healthy masculine is intensely loving. Indeed, love transcends the polarities and is a *human* quality. The primary way the masculine loves is through committing and cherishing. This level of devotion means that the masculine man remains committed to his partner, his family, his ideals, his values…to the sacrifice of all else. And he is deeply devoted and cherishes his intimate feminine partner by honoring her emotions above his own and by *never leaving her alone in her pain until a solution can be reached*. He is committed to resolving his partner's pain or discomfort through his ideas, logic, and action.

Outdated notions of the masculine typically feature emotionless stoicism. What this emotionally sterile model leaves out is a *critical quality* of masculinity, which is nurturing. We often think of nurturing as a feminine quality, but in fact, *nurturing* is defined as encouraging growth and development, which are intrinsically masculine traits. That's right, men in their balanced and thriving masculinity are always encouraging the healthy growth and development of their relationships, their children and family members, their partners, their careers…you name it. Think about wise masculine characters such as Gandalf, Obi-Wan Kenobi, or Morpheus. Those are the kind of nurturers the healthy masculine becomes: the kind who fosters heroes and world-saving adventures.

Of course, our men live in this modern-day world, too. One where traditional roles are being (rightly) questioned and more options are available. Gone is the notion of the man being absent from the home, a heartless robot simply meant to pay the bills. Today, men have choices, just like women do, to participate more fully in their own lives, families, and life trajectories. No longer do they have the societal requirement to hold the same job for thirty-five years only to retire and then slowly wither. No longer are they expected to be the harsh disciplinarian to the children when they return home from a long day of work. No longer are they relegated to being emotionless "boys who don't cry."

Real men do cry. In fact, healthy men embrace the feminine aspects within them. When emotions run high, they look to their feminine partner to comfort them…but they don't leave their feminine partner in the masculine nurturing role forever. They use the support and the space to properly process their emotions, work through them with their partner (or family or therapist), and then reorient themselves to their essential masculine nature. Fully developed healthy masculine men always return to themselves and never abandon their feminine counterparts to don the masculine mask permanently.

Balanced and healthy masculine men want to be respected for who they are: for their clear decisions and leadership, their delightful generosity, their clever ideas, and their proud contributions.

For feminine women, it is easiest for us to respect these men when we are confident that they have our best interests at heart, whether they be our intimate partner, family member, colleague, ally, or community member. Wherever we find masculine men, may they cherish the highest needs of the feminine and remain in symbiotic balance with her.

The Power and Purpose of Feminine Intuition

One of the greatest gifts of the feminine polarity is intuition. Ladies, we all have it. But, as I've said earlier, intuition is often deemed dangerous. Even as little girls, we are told of the witches of yore who were both revered and reviled for their intuition. It was feared because it sometimes bordered on fortune-telling. Women were vilified for their intuitive sense of the world around them; at the worst of times, they were burned at the stake.

In today's world, while there may be no more literal witch hunts, women's intuition is still shunned and thought of as illogical — because the masculine prizes logic so highly and that is the dominant cultural paradigm. When questioned repeatedly about our intuitive guidance, we women often resort to second-guessing our intuition, or else we shut it off completely. This cuts us off from the divine providence that is inherently ours.

Our secret gift, the intuition that drives us on a soul level is powerful, primal, and right. We feel it in our gut. Studies even reveal that the chemicals of emotion are made in our stomachs: this is the physical location of our gut brain and the driver of our best intuitive decision-making.

Sure, logic is handy at times. And there's no harm in weighing some logic against an intuitive hit. But in the end, we always suffer if we go against our gut in favor of a more masculine, logic-driven decision. Not everything in life inspires an inner knowing...but the things that do? Better to pay attention.

The more attention you pay to your intuition, the more in

alignment you are with what is right and good and true for you. Being in that kind of intuitive alignment is what keeps us in our feminine polarity. It's what keeps us thriving, flourishing, happy, and in the flow of grace and gratitude every day.

When our intuition is questioned (or we question it ourselves) or challenged (or we challenge it ourselves), it diminishes our trust in the feminine power within us. We lose our guidance system. We lose our creativity, our imagination, and our self-expressiveness. Dare I say it, but we lose ourselves.

Our intuitive guidance has been honed through a long lineage of our foremothers since time immemorial. Your grandmother gave it to your mother, and your mother gave it to you. There were things that they learned, saw, felt, touched, tasted, and experienced that helped them to wield what was wildly powerful inside them. Through the power of that lineage, you own the rights to that wisdom and are charged with wielding it now, in your time.

That is not a lofty proclamation. Epigenetics tells us that experiences our ancestors had may be passed down to us at a genetic level. Intuition is that fundamental.

When your grandmother walked across broken glass to plant your family in a new country, her soul spoke to yours across time. She gave you a home. She informed your sense of place and being and rightness. That is a powerful teaching. It is your job, granddaughter, to heed it.

When your intuition speaks, imagine it is your beloved ancestor whispering in your ear exactly what you need to hear.

I was lucky enough to have a sacred and life-altering relationship with my precious grandmother. She was born in Ukraine and taken from her family by German soldiers at the age of fourteen, only to survive the Second World War in a prison camp. She then languished as a refugee in Germany for thirteen years, until she had the opportunity to immigrate to the United States. The time and circumstances of her life meant that she wasn't able to make many choices about what was best for her. Events were forced upon her that were out of her control, and as a result, she never faltered in encouraging me to lean into my gifts, exercise my own agency, and live life on my own terms.

I grew up with those lessons. With her words in my ear about how important it was to live your truth. To pursue what makes you happy. And to never let anyone diminish your spark.

In fact, a few years after my grandfather died, when I'd come to her home to take care of her and spend some time with her, I presented her with a career opportunity I had been given that required me to move to New York City. I was concerned about leaving her all alone and how much I would miss her. My whole life, I knew how precious she and my grandfather were to me, and I never took them for granted. When I explained my situation, without hesitation she told me to go. She reminded me that she would have loved the option to pursue a career as a young woman, and she was honored I was being given the chance — the choice — to do so myself. She told me that through pursuing the fullness of my own life, I would honor her presence in mine.

When my intuition speaks up, I imagine it's her voice connecting through time and space to reach me here and now and remind me of who I am. In fact, I have heard her voice in my darkest times when I've pondered what step to take next.

She's never far from my heart. Years after her passing, I found myself in a difficult situation in my intimate relationship, questioning whether to continue with it or not. Sitting at my dining table in tears, ready to end it all and walk away, I heard her say to me as clearly as if she was standing next to me: "Stick with him. He loves you." I have never doubted her words, and so I did stick with him.

If you didn't have such a close relationship with a female elder, then I hope you'll pay attention to the next best thing: your own intuitive knowing.

Women in your deep history cared about you enough to pass

down their message and placed it in your soul so you would listen when it mattered most. Of course it's hard. I know it's hard. We're women. Our choices are never easy.

But they are necessary. Thank goodness we live in a time when we have choice. I firmly believe that the greatest lesson my grandmother allowed me to recognize was that she lived a life where she didn't have choices so that I could live a life where I make my own.

That's an incredible legacy.

It's not only my legacy. It's yours, too.

Own it.

The next time your intuition bubbles up from the depth of your being: listen. When it whispers, "You've got this," then go ahead and get it. When it screams, "Stop right now," then halt like you're approaching a thousand-foot cliff. And when it says, "Get out," well, then you leave immediately.

Your intuition also encourages you to love harder, open more, and stay the course. And your intuitive whispering doesn't initially have to make any sense. The directions may not always be what we expect, and they may not always be easy to follow. However, they are always worth it, and they always guide us in the direction of our highest good.

The Needs of the Satisfied Woman

Now that we have a clearer understanding of the psychic polarities, which one we most comfortably and primarily express, and some basic foundations of what it means to be the Satisfied Woman, I want to turn to what the Satisfied Woman needs.

Because, as the feminine, we have great needs. And we always want *more*.

We are not greedy, and we are not out of hand. Our constant desire for more comes from a place of continual recalibration — or perhaps you might say dissatisfaction. If I could coolly include a wink emoji here in this book and not diminish the impact of the delivery, I certainly would! Our dissatisfaction is not driven by malcontentedness or contempt. And it does not mean that we are never satisfied. Of course we are — after all, the premise of this book is finding our way as the Satisfied Woman.

Being comfortable with the needs of the feminine and the innate desire for more requires us to also be comfortable with change. Flux. Flow. Fluidity. In fact, the only constant in the universe is change, and this is the domain of the feminine. Look at our bodies, for example. We undertake incredible biological changes at several critical periods in our life: puberty, with the growth of life-giving breasts and the significance of menstruation; pregnancy (if we choose it) and the ability to grow and nurture a human being to term; and menopause, with the dramatic cessation of our ability to provide life via our bodies. Comparatively speaking, men don't undertake changes like these! Women even experience big changes every month with their menstrual and hormonal cycles.

Our entire existence is based upon being comfortable with big shifts and great change. And all those shifts and changes mean that something that may have given us respite a few weeks ago is now no longer helpful. Or it may mean that what we once accepted as perfect conditions actually need to be…well, further perfected. Think of your body as a barometer measuring the climate not just of your household but of your career, your relationships, your family, your daily habits — everything.

And within this miraculously ever-changing body is your greatest gift: your intuition. Your intuition serves you as the means to know when things need to budge just a little or to come crashing down altogether. Your intuitive guidance urges you to seek more comfort in all aspects of your life. In fact, one of my favorite questions to ask girlfriends is this: "Are you comfortable? OK, then. How could you be *more* comfortable?"

Let's lean into the feminine need for more. It doesn't have to be over-the-top, garish, or expensive. It doesn't have to be demanding, be demeaning, or put people out. It is just exactly what we need in the moment to create the greatest *satisfaction* possible. What is also true is that when women find satisfaction, so does everyone around them. The healthy feminine is confident enough in her intuitive knowing and emotional well-being to seek satisfaction in all ways possible for herself and those around her. And the healthy masculine is inspired to address the intuitive needs of his feminine counterpart in order to boost her comfort and satisfaction. (How he goes about it may be a curiosity, but with patience, he gets there in the end.)

While I can't give a list of items or conditions that satisfy all women — let's be honest, in today's highly unique and individualized culture, all things are awesomely OK for a woman to desire — what I can provide is a list of *qualities*, or Four Keys, that the Satisfied Woman possesses. As you'll recall from earlier in this chapter, the Four Keys are safety, security, trust, and being cherished.

When these Four Keys are present, it is easy for the Satisfied Woman to relax completely into her femininity. She can take a deep breath knowing that her sense of *safety* and *security* are met. She can surrender to her environment because she *trusts* it completely. And she can experience the fullness of pleasure in her body when she is utterly *cherished*.

Breathe into that, satisfied sister. This is what I want for you. For all of us.

These keys warrant a deeper examination, as they give us the structure for all the needs we may want to have met in our satisfied lives. Now, the outward variations of this structure may look wildly different for each of us. I am certainly grateful that we live in a time and place where safety doesn't only mean a woman living a restricted life in a house with a family, and security doesn't only mean having a husband at work earning all the money to pay the bills. I couldn't be more relieved that trust isn't forcibly taken by another simply because he is a man or that pleasure isn't forced or faked because of how women *think* they are supposed to respond in the bedroom. And it is heartening to think that women can finally be cherished for their power and agency, and not just when they are meek and diminutive toward their masculine counterpart. We have freedom to be feminine. In whatever way we choose.

What we need to be mindful of is curating a life for ourselves where these Four Keys are present in as many areas as possible. While I defined the nature of the qualities earlier, you get to determine how they manifest for you in your wildly feminine life. For example, for you, safety may extend beyond mere physical safety and the ability to be free from harm and include also a desire for privacy by not engaging in social media. Security may go beyond having a rocking 401(k) account and stock options and mean that you have a level of commitment from a loving partner that gives you confidence in your collaborative life together. It is possible for the Four Keys to find expression in physical, mental, emotional, relational, and spiritual ways. Trust may extend beyond those you feel you "should" trust (like genetic family) and be given freely to a family of your choosing. While cherishing is defined as the masculine's ability to honor your emotions and intuition above his own and make choices accordingly, *you* get to decide how you most love to be cherished: Does he run you a daily bath? Support your burgeoning career? Give you quiet solitude when you feel melancholy?

No matter what your needs are, it is critical that they be met. I know you know what it is like when you have an unmet need. For us as women, it is an intolerable state that digs away at our soul and creates an inner tension that spills into our daily life. Leave this need unmet for too long, and it becomes consuming, divisive, and distorting. It causes consternation within family, disconnection in relationship, and, at its very worst, resentment in you. I like to say that resentment is the relationship killer, but really, resentment is the everything killer.

When an unmet need festers into resentment, that means we have crossed the Rubicon of repair and can't go back to resolve what was unmet in the first place. The unmet need for cleanliness, for example, may mean that towels left on the floor eventually cause resentment and (surprisingly for your partner) lead to an outburst that is clearly disproportionate to the problem. When unmet needs are unaddressed, the molehills turn into mountains, the hurt gets buried in the body and turns into physical ailments, and the minor annoyance eventually results in a nasty breakup.

Getting our needs met is *critical.* Whether we seek to meet our own needs or have those valuable people in our lives help us to achieve them, it is imperative that they are met. Focus on taking stock of your life, seeing where the Four Keys are present and where they are not, and identify what you need to change, erase, or enhance. Every expression of your unique life is awesomely OK — as long as you choose it. As long as it meets your needs. And as long as it features these Four Keys.

With the Four Keys as the foundation for leading a satisfied life, you can now look with your feminine eyes on the life you have before you and make (perhaps exacting) decisions on what stays and what goes. You can determine what you need more of and what you need less of. Listen to the intuition from within that inspires spiritual, emotional, and physical housecleaning. Let yourself be constantly recalibrated. Comfort with change, always wanting more, and fiercely protecting our needs are built into our womanly form. Now, let's embrace these qualities, honor them, and live them as the Satisfied Woman.

3

Permission to Disrupt

It's no secret that we live in a patriarchal society that values power over empowerment, dominion over communion, and control over contentment. This culture that we live in developed over many millennia to assert and affirm those in power: namely, men and male-dominated paradigms.

Let me be exceedingly clear here.

All men are not our enemy. The masculine is not the sole source of our pain.

Men whose masculine energy is misaligned within them and expresses its distorted attributes are our challenge. Those who do not see the grace in cohabitating and cocreating a world alongside the feminine reinforce unbalanced paradigms. Men who have had no training or leadership in how to express healthy masculine traits contribute to the patriarchy. And those who are scared to express their courageous masculine play small so as not to be our allies.

We need to find our allies.

They are out there. Good men. Strong men. Not strong in the sense of He-Man. Rather, strong in their leadership, protection, contribution, logic, and presence. Strong in the generous ways that the feminine needs and that provide balance to this sacred duality.

Strong in their integrity by always ensuring that their good intentions and their actions are unwaveringly aligned. Strong in their protectorship of and partnership with the feminine.

The Patriarchal Condition

Unfortunately, cultural, patriarchal, societal, and familial trauma has been perpetrated on the feminine for a very long time. Be aware: this is not a blame game. Blame is merely a way to outsource pain and shame and mire ourselves in victimhood. There are no victims in a state of empowerment. From this perspective, it is possible to take an objective look at conditions that have created some of the more common difficulties women face: namely, the challenges to disrupting the current paradigm and questioning the status quo in order to bring about a healthier expression of the human polarities at every level of personal and interpersonal life.

On a macro level, and simply put, patriarchy seeks to oppress femininity and exert *power over* women. In a structure like this, balance and equality are virtually impossible to achieve. Anytime we find a hierarchy, we also find a power imbalance. Both masculinity and femininity are powerful *on their own terms*, and outside of hierarchy they are able to find great *power with* each other by expressing their unique strengths. Unfortunately, patriarchy is insidious; it is difficult to find a contemporary cultural scenario that isn't infused with it.

Even if I tried to highlight professions that are dominated by women, such as the health care and the yoga industries, I could easily find examples in them where women earn less than men, are taken advantage of through uncompensated time, and are bullied into submission by male superiors. I wish I could name a religious institution that achieves a beautiful balance, except many systems still do not allow for female clergy, and religions still exist that actively subjugate women to the point of removing their ability to have any independence.

Again, I would love to be wrong about this point. I'm happy for a reader to connect with me and share a tale of a balanced social structure that empowers and enhances masculinity and femininity equally. In fact, I would love to present that to everyone in my community as a shining example. In lieu of that, perhaps our best chance of creating the most optimal conditions for us to lean into and be valued for our femininity is through our own personal, private relationships with those around us. Because there *are* good men out there, and there *are* allies who value the feminine. If you find one, you know it, because they prioritize, protect, and enhance the Four Keys on your behalf. In return, you offer them respect, inspiration, creativity, joy, and receptivity. And together you achieve a balance that allows everyone to thrive — and you to be the Satisfied Woman.

Taking Back the Crazy Train

One of the most harmful weapons of the patriarchy is the rejection and suppression of the most powerful gifts of femininity: our intuition and our emotions. These exist beyond logic, in the realm of the unconscious, which doesn't need to be understood but rather is felt authentically and meaningfully by the feminine. Our intuition and emotions often prompt us to question the status quo and catalyze change, making these gifts of ours dangerous for the distorted masculine in power.

In order to mitigate the potentially disruptive effects of a woman's intuitive feelings and questions, they are vilified, ridiculed, and doubted. What woman hasn't heard — even from people who love her — admonishments like:

You're being illogical.
You don't understand what you're like.

You're making this up in your head.
You should feel X about Y.
You're crazy.

The worst one yet. And no, we're not crazy.

Calling women crazy is nothing new. For millennia, this type of gaslighting has been the basis of suppression, repression, subversion, subjugation, and worse. It's a method of moving women into a disempowered and destabilized position — and it is very effective.

If you have taken any psychology courses, you have likely heard that the clinical diagnosis of "hysteria" used to be reserved for women whose perceptions of life were unreconcilable with what they were told was reality. When a woman's behavior was disagreeable, she was said to be "hysterical" and treated through the application of sex or sexual energy from a man (even by a doctor!). Seriously. A man's digital clitoral stimulation or the penetrative application of his semen was thought to be the healing force a woman needed to bring her around to logic and reason — that is, a man's way of thinking.

The Greeks and Romans coined the term *hysteria*, literally meaning "wandering womb," and blamed a woman's uterus for moving uncontrollably within her body and inspiring any number of ailments — anger, depression, argumentativeness, melancholy, fits, fainting. No matter what was wrong with a woman, she was labeled hysterical and subjected to correction. This became formalized within the field of psychology in the 1880s — and lasted as a legitimate diagnosis until 1980.

This means that even within the past generation, the disorders and distress of a woman were dismissed as a medical problem caused by the simple fact that she had a uterus. Her complaints were neither heard nor addressed, and any objections from her were called "crazy."

Being called crazy makes us *feel* like we are crazy, especially when the criticism comes from people we love and trust. Why would the people in our lives doubt our emotions, intuition, and needs that arise from these gifts if they were true? They must be right, right? Well, our intuitions and emotions are *always true for us.* Always. They are critically important signals directing us to our best decisions, our highest good, and our greatest satisfaction. When those signals are in a direction other than the linear one preset by the masculine paradigm around us, then the easiest solution to shutting those signals down is to resort to gaslighting and the (over)use of terms like *crazy.*

So we are often convinced that our intuition is wrong and not to be trusted, that our emotions are invalid or scary, that our desires are incorrect, and that our dreams are misplaced. We learn little by little (or sometimes in catastrophic ways) to second-guess ourselves and to believe that our own inbuilt guidance system cannot be relied upon. Unfortunately, *it is actually crazy making* when we doubt our own soul's intuitive messages and desires. It causes us to allow others to dictate what they think we need. We become convinced that unhealthy situations are tolerable. And we forgo the feeling of safety and security we need by fooling ourselves into believing that our partners or family have our back.

The label of "crazy" and related efforts to make women doubt their feminine strengths have worked all too well for the patriarchy as it cows us into submission and restrains our voices and questions so that we (unwillingly and uncomfortably) accept the status quo and believe what we are told rather than what we feel. This strategy works well when we are disempowered and entrenched in a hierarchical system.

It's time to rise up like all the female inquisitors before us and start questioning: questioning what feels uncomfortable, inequitable, untrustworthy, unsafe, and uncherished. It's time to question all the things that fly in the face of our fierce intuition and feminine knowing. When your soul speaks in emotions and your psyche delivers an intuitive hit, it is time to follow that thread, like the Greek myth of Ariadne winding through the maze to root out the Minotaur.

The half-man, half-bull Minotaur is the creature that represents all the shadow within our unconscious. He is our greatest fears, all we deny or repress, and that which we have yet to understand about ourselves. The maze is our psyche, with its twists and turns and nonsensical, nonlinear structure. Within the maze we find hidden our dreams, urges, pain, traumas, and truths. Those shadow elements are not faulty or worthy of being destroyed or sacrificed, as Ariadne's lover Theseus (in his brazen masculinity) so desperately tries to do. We cannot chase the Minotaur to the center of the maze and use our logical, straight-edged masculine sword to hack it to bits. The beast is the friend of the feminine (as bull iconography often was in ancient cultures), and she makes the Minotaur her ally with her inquisitive nature.

Most importantly, she pacifies it with her desire to inhabit the darkest reaches of the underworld as she sacrifices fear for love and sees the beast for what it is: a misunderstood part of her, locked away and dreaded simply because it is unknown. Knowledge is power. The mythical Ariadne knows the power and value of all that lies within the maze. For the satisfied woman, this translates to leaning into the feminine realm of the unconscious, diving into the darkness of the psyche, and honoring all that is feared by engaging in endless, relentless questioning.

Our intuition is basic, primitive…animalian. Consider it our inner Minotaur, that beast feared by the masculine, befriended by the feminine, and formed out of inner truths so powerful they cannot be ignored. Neither can our intuition. It is the source of our greatest strength. Intuition is our inner wisdom. It offers the potential of release from suffering, as suffering is always caused by the unquestioned mind — or the unbefriended Minotaur. As the feminine, we are uniquely equipped to be empowered by it, making it our ally in the pursuit of what supports our health, healing, well-being, and vibrancy.

Follow that sacred thread into the maze of your own unconscious. What you find there is powerful, immutable, and tamable
only by your befriending and honoring of it.

A Woman's Inquisition

Throughout history, women have been disrupters. We are the
questioners. We are inquisitive by nature, and our feminine intuition gives us a deep spidey sense, the ability to sniff out situations
that don't satisfy our need for safety or security. Things sometimes
just feel wrong, and when we can't put our finger on it, when we
can't trust it, we go digging. We pick at the wound or the pustule
until it bursts, revealing its malignant origins.

Gross, I know. But *this* is a woman's work.

Forget the kitchen. A woman's work is addressing the healthy
balance of life all around her. I don't mean this in a strictly literal
sense, either. It doesn't require the physical birthing of children or
the tough choices required for an elder family member in hospice.
Women seek life energy in all circumstances: that fecund, fertile
soil in which our joy, hopes, dreams, and creativity flourish.

Women are uniquely designed to be the harbingers of both
life and death. As Joseph Campbell referenced it, women are both
"the womb and the tomb." We are just as well adjusted to support
life-giving as we are to offer palliative care to whomever or whatever needs it. Consider the natural instincts of animal mothers that
kill their own young if they are unable to survive in the wild. As
women, we are also the brave ones who may snuff out the life force
of something — an idea, a circumstance, a relationship — that
can't be adequately sustained.

As naturally as an animal seeks out just the right substrate to
make a home, women both crave and need conditions that provide
us with the Four Keys of femininity: safety, security, trust, and the
ability to be cherished. We know that when these Four Keys are
present, we enjoy the life-affirming energy of harmony, peace, and

ease all around us and extending to everyone in our orbit. These keys unlock the doors of vibrant and vital living. When the Four Keys are not present, the sense of discomfort within a woman's body is so persistent that it cannot be ignored.

That sense of discomfort, the inner knowing that a situation is not safe, or that she is not cherished, or that any one of the Four Keys is not present, does not abate until it is addressed. It is very likely that the stress creeps out through the physical body. It may just be a little butterfly in the stomach, or perhaps it manifests as a headache or a rash. One thing is for certain: when a woman starts to question the conditions and circumstances she is in, the questions do not magically go away.

Those questions demand answers.

Whether we ask the questions of ourselves or of those around us; whether we're questioning the culture, framework, or doctrine we find ourselves in; whether we're questioning the world or our place in it, the feminine mind, heart, and intuition do not settle until they have found a satisfactory answer.

Think about our foremothers who were labeled as witches and burned at the stake. Their questions came at a time and in a place where oppression was so strong and fierce and the fear around destabilizing the patriarchal status quo was so great that sacrifice was the only option. Consider Joan of Arc, whose bravery was heralded as she intuitively and through divine inspiration guided the French army to victory and who was then martyred for voicing the same inner truth that had enabled her to lead them…and for wearing men's clothing.

Women learn early on that speaking up is dangerous business. Voicing our intuition, our inner truths, our divine connections often has consequences. Those consequences don't need to be as dire as out-and-out martyrdom to feel both dramatic and traumatic. Just being told to shut up can stifle our glorious voice. Being gaslit to believe what we think or feel is inherently wrong makes us question our own sense of self. Not being heard and believed by those we love is often enough to make our questions stop in our throats before they are even voiced.

This has repercussions. When a woman isn't allowed to question her condition in order to instigate change, she is then stuck in a condition that is uninhabitable and drains her of life energy. The resulting physical, psychological, emotional, and spiritual stress has lasting effects when left unaddressed. Physician and author Gabor Maté's body of work centers around the physical ailments that are generated through psychological stress and trauma. In his book *When the Body Says No*, he asserts that what is important is not the type of trauma that we experience but, rather, what happens inside our bodies and minds as a result of this trauma.

I think many of us know intrinsically that our traumas and circumstances play a major role in our physical and mental well-being. I came to this realization fairly early on in my struggles with Hashimoto's thyroiditis. In fact, I remember a specific traumatic incident at the age of fourteen, when my father, in an alcoholic, narcissistic rage, yelled at me to shut up and then proceeded to berate me with a litany of verbal slanders that I could not counter or defend against. I remember my throat feeling hot and swelling up for the first time, becoming so prominent that my father even noticed it amid his tirade.

Through my journey of healing and discovery with this auto-immune disorder, it became abundantly clear that my thyroid was like the signal flag on a vessel hailing the condition of the boat to port. When I was in a safe place, free to be myself, my autoimmune disorder and thyroid relaxed. When I was in an acutely stressful situation, my thyroid would swell and throb, my neck would get red and hot, and my autoimmune issue would flare. I came to learn over two decades with this illness that my exterior condition contributed as much as my interior condition to my happiness and health.

Unfortunately, as a young woman I didn't have the tools to foster health from any angle. Western medicine hadn't caught up to the wisdom of functional medicine, which points to myriad underlying triggers for autoimmunity, and I had not had adequate time to integrate my own explorations of spirituality and psychology, which assist in methods of self-inquiry and emphasize emotional well-being. Perhaps most importantly, even though I had an innate discomfort about my condition and surroundings, I was not in a position to question them, much less to get my questions answered. It took more than a decade for me to develop the confidence in my intuition and the agency to follow it and to finally take back my own health. It is only through fierce questioning that we find the answers we need.

A woman's inquisition is perhaps as important as her feminine intuition. At the very least, they go hand in hand. Our internal intuitive guidance system leads us toward what brings us most closely into alignment with our true nature and allows us to relax into the feminine polarity. Without the questioning, we remain in conditions that perpetuate instability and unease (or even disease) and bring us out of alignment with our authenticity. Even if our intuition suggests that a situation is not right for us, without proper follow-up inquiry, we may never discover what *is* right for us. We may never raise the red flags of unmet needs, unsafe conditions, unfulfilled desires, or unacceptable interactions.

Think about how children do this regularly. Children under about ten years old are all entirely in the feminine polarity. They are receptive, playful, pleasure-seeking, and in need of leadership, protection, support, safety, and cherishing. They rely on their caregivers to provide for all their needs. And a hallmark of children? Questioning the very nature of everything.

They do this not just to learn about the world around them but to discover the motivations of the people in their lives, test boundaries of what is possible, and ensure that their needs are being met. When children are admonished for questioning, the stifling of that inquiry leads them to have a skewed understanding of their world, perplexity about appropriate behavior (for themselves and others), and a misknowing of reality. Think about the age-old parental adage "Do what I say, not what I do." If a child heeds this, then they'll feel confusion around actions, intentions, and motivations. Not to mention further confusion about how they should behave in similar situations in the future.

Children understand on a soul level that to find out more about their world and their place in it, they must question. As women, we must lean into our own questions as well. The questions come from deep within our feminine soul, the part of us that needs the Four Keys in order to flourish and that desires the freedom and confidence to be wildly, unabashedly satisfied.

Making Shift Happen

When women question their surroundings, their relationships, or their reality, their inquiry is often in conflict with how others perceive a situation. The masculine desires stability and the status quo, and it initially resists change — or disruption. If things are "working fine," then the masculine fiercely holds on to the existing state of affairs. This is true in the culture, in the workplace, in religion, in relationship, in anything that has a prior process or expectation. The masculine seeks to lead, to direct, and to stay on the given path — sometimes come hell or high water.

This kind of persistence and fortitude is a gift and a true strength of the healthy masculine. Perseverance against discomfort to overcome odds is what gets us to the finish line on almost anything we can imagine. And if the point of an action is to reach a goal, then the linear, masculine way of working is ideal.

But life isn't linear. Journeys are circuitous, circling back on themselves, diverging in a wood, pausing for a much-needed rest. That circuitousness is very much of the feminine. Even the most well-prepared journeyer must change their trajectory once in a while. Sometimes a perfectly planned route needs a GPS update. We have all become accustomed to navigation apps like Waze or

Google Maps rerouting our travels because of unforeseen traffic or roadwork. We need that same flexibility in life as well.

Because things do change. We get more information. Or motivations shift. In any of these circumstances, the change is felt first by the feminine. Her sensitive and intuitive nature feels the discomfort or the disruption. It starts as a nagging in our insides, pulling at us to do something differently. We must trust that intuition.

And we must be cherished enough *to be heard* when things need to shift.

The good thing about the masculine ability to lead and pursue a course of action is that it can always pursue a new course. It is in getting the masculine to realize a new course is necessary where the feminine finds trouble. For the masculine, it's generally easier to just carry on as intended. This may mean an internal come-to-Jesus moment about heeding your feminine intuition over the plans your inner masculine has already made. Or it may mean communicating your intuitive needs to a masculine friend, relative, or partner. Although any man who hasn't listened to a woman's needs finds out really quickly that there is nothing easier about that! Her sense of disruption expresses itself as gentle questioning at first…and then escalates into fierce inquiry as time marches on and her needs are not met.

The urgency of a woman's intuition pulling at her soul spills over into interpersonal relationships as well as social, professional, and collective relationships and circumstances. The necessity for the feminine to have comfort and safety cannot be underestimated or ignored. When it is, there are consequences for both the masculine and the feminine: the feminine is undermined and repressed, while the masculine attempts to either dismiss or exert control over the feminine. This results in imbalance and disconnection, a state that is disturbing to both polarities. From this destabilized place, the feminine is often misunderstood and unfortunately mislabeled as crazy. While it sometimes *feels* easier to label a woman as crazy or gaslight her into believing she's wrong than it is to just address the source of discomfort and fix the problem, it is truly not easier for anyone and always results in incredible dissatisfaction.

Intuition Drives Satisfaction

The stress of dissatisfaction cuts deep. At first, it may just impair joy, but eventually it moves past sadness or anger and grows into resentment. As soon as we hit resentment, we've crossed the point of no return. Resentment is a relationship killer, whether it's directed toward the relationship we have with ourselves or toward someone else who seems unable to have our highest good in mind. In order to avoid the road to resentment, we need to address dissatisfaction quickly — as soon as our intuition turns into inquisition.

Our intuitive feelings are not simply our greatest gift, they are the *drivers of satisfaction*. When we listen to our intuition and honor our feelings, we are more easily able to understand our needs and get them met. Getting our needs met and doing our best to establish a foundation with the Four Keys in our life is perhaps both the most basic goal and the highest aim of the Satisfied Woman. Almost all our needs in every area of our life have at their core one of the elements of the Four Keys. So, while we are all unique individual women, expressing ourselves in the myriad glorious ways possible, we are all bonded through these Four Keys of feminine satisfaction. They are at the heart of all our wishes and needs!

Identifying your needs is a crucial element for leading life as the Satisfied Woman. Understanding how a need correlates to one of the Four Keys helps you become clear on its importance and why having that need met allows you to lean into your true feminine essence. Your being able to communicate that need and its associated key gives the masculine a greater understanding and urgency to help you get that need met. Each polarity thrives when the needs of both are met, whether the masculine we're talking about is that part of your own psyche (for example, when you justify to your masculine side a purchase based on the need of your feminine side so that all parts of you feel good about it), or a relationship with a masculine partner (as when you establish personal relationship boundaries that keep you both in your appropriate polarities), or ensuring you're a part of social structures that enhance and enliven your feminine (for instance, by quitting a job that is rife with inequality).

So the needs of the feminine are driven by feeling and intuition and are underpinned by the Four Keys. The highest expression of the masculine toward the feminine is to cherish those feelings and make excellent decisions, with her highest good in mind, that help get her needs met. But the healthy masculine cannot do this in a vacuum, nor can the masculine read minds! The feminine must communicate clearly to have a hope of getting her needs met.

This means we have to speak up. And not in the way that is stereotypically expected of the feminine...that circuitous fashion that asks for things without asking at all. If we are to be understood by the healthy masculine, and if the masculine is to honor our needs from a loving, wholehearted place, then we need to communicate clearly. Remember, this is most possible with the healthy expression of the masculine *and* the feminine, as either polarity in distortion may not be able to get needs met in a wholehearted fashion.

To determine and describe a feminine need, first consider how one of the Four Keys is supported or enhanced by it. Here are some examples:

- **Safety:** "To enhance my feeling of safety, I need to make sure this job provides the right benefits."
- **Security:** "In order for me to feel secure in this relationship, I need a greater, more formalized level of commitment."
- **Trust:** "I feel like I can trust you when you stay in integrity and follow through on your word."
- **To be cherished:** "It really shows you cherish me when

you go out of your way to find my favorite thing or do my favorite activity."

While those examples all seem fairly simple, what I want to demonstrate here is that clearly determining and describing your needs *is* a simplistic formula. When you can identify the heart of the need with one of the Four Keys, then it becomes easier not only for you to state the need but for your counterpart to understand its importance to you.

Importance, of course, is a funny thing. What is important to one person may be inane to another. I remember hearing a friend of mine describe an argument with his wife where the color of the paint in the kitchen was the clincher. He was not fussed about the color, but the level of importance to her was great, and when he balked at the color she wanted because it had a higher price point, things turned sour. For him, the importance lay in the cost. For her, the importance lay in the aesthetic. In cases like this, there is no "winning" side. But both sides lose when the perceived importance isn't understood or, worse, is diminished in the other person's eyes.

If your boss doesn't know how important it is to you that your off hours and vacation time be honored so that you can feel safe in the job, then that must be clearly communicated. If your partner can't understand your need to always have the refrigerator properly stocked to fulfill your sense of security, then speak that out loud. And when those around you or the circumstances you find yourself in do not meet your needs, then it may be time to reassess your situation. Let your intuition guide you in knowing whether more patience is required or whether your needs are simply not being honored. This is where boundaries come in handy.

A couple of key things to understand about boundaries are (1) that they simply reflect your soul's clear yes or clear no on an issue and (2) that they are for you to uphold for yourself. This means that when your soul cries out with an unequivocal "Yes!"

or "No!," then you've found a boundary that you need to apply. Letting boundaries slip or be moving targets is not only confusing but potentially dangerous. Like the borders of a playground for children, boundaries keep everyone safe and allow the full field to be explored. Without those fences, children tend to group in the middle, unsure of where they can play without harm or where they might be wandering off into unknown territory.

The same idea applies to us as feminine women. When we are clear on our boundaries and reinforce them with our own actions, it sets us up for greater safety, security, and the ability to trust and be cherished. This became painfully apparent at a long-ago brunch date with a friend of mine whose relationship had devolved to her partner having multiple affairs with her colleagues. We worked in the same field, and unfortunately, everyone was aware of her partner's indiscretions, adding public humiliation to the insult and injury. During our time together, she shared how painful this experience was for her and how upsetting it was that her boundaries around fidelity and monogamy were completely ignored. She complained, "I've said over and over that I can't trust him unless he is faithful to me. He needs to stop sleeping with other women!" When I explained to her that her boundaries are for *her* to uphold, she found it very difficult to hear.

Her desire for fidelity meant that she was hoping to get her intimate partner to honor her boundaries by changing *his* ways. Unfortunately, we can't change other people! If, for whatever reason, they are unable or unwilling to help us get our needs met or work with our boundaries, then our duty to our own souls is to honor our personal boundaries ourselves. This means we need to decide whether a situation is worth a little more patience or whether it is time to walk away.

Keeping our boundaries clear is one way we help others understand what is important to us and how we want to be treated in any type of relationship (including the one with ourselves). When boundaries blur — when we forgive the cheater, overlook the demeaning comments, gloss over transgressions — the expectation then becomes that we accept that type of behavior and that our needs are not valuable. For too long in history, the expectation has been that it is reasonable to walk all over women's needs, wants, and desires. So much so that even we, as women, subjugate our own needs and martyr ourselves for others. All. The. Time. We don't speak up when the family carpool schedule becomes too demanding. We suffer in an uncommitted relationship just hoping the other person will finally finalize their divorce. We let the boss dictate our hours or job responsibilities without mentioning prior plans.

Somewhere in the history of this patriarchal culture, the needs of women have been deemed unimportant and unnecessary. It's up to us to stop *believing* this narrative, and it starts by reclaiming trust in our own intuitive emotions. When a situation doesn't feel right, then it is time to start the inquest. When our questions need answering, we frame them in such a way that clearly states the need, and we reinforce it with our own acceptable boundaries. In order for us to do our best to set the foundation of the Four Keys in our life and have the greatest chance at expressing our fullest femininity, we start by listening to the messages of our soul. They are there, satisfied sister. Tune in and let your intuition be your guide to life as the Satisfied Woman.

Gracefully (and Gratefully) Uneasy

Finding a way to draw attention to unease is no easy task. The unease we experience when something just *doesn't feel right* is nagging, unending, and unforgiving. As feminine women, we have all felt it. We have all been in circumstances where our intuition wells up from our soul and offers a warning. Whether we heed it or not determines our ultimate well-being.

The patriarchy may say this is an overly dramatic statement, but it's not. We feminine women know the discomfort we feel when we don't listen to the call of our inner knowing — whether for good or for bad! It may be reaching out to signal that we have found someone important in our lives, but we second-guess that feeling and miss the opportunity for deep connection. Or it may be reaching out to warn us that something isn't OK in our world, and if we don't speak up to correct the course, then we suffer all the more for it.

While my many years of research, study, and scholarship in this field have continually affirmed the importance of listening to our intuitive guidance, this point was brought home to me in a powerful way very recently. One morning, my beloved masculine partner was preparing to head out on a motorcycle ride and leave me to write for the day. This is a fairly regular occurrence and not something I ever balk at, because I love this for both of us. It serves my need to put words on a page and his need to feel the freedom of the open road.

But on this particular morning, something didn't feel right, and my intuition was screaming. I couldn't put my finger on it and wasn't able to articulate any particular incident that was causing my anxiety and worry. In my emotional confusion, I just followed him around the house repeating, "Don't go. I wish you wouldn't go." Being the masculine, he kept asking for reasons, but I didn't have a rational understanding yet. He tried to reassure me and continued to get ready, but the reassurance only heightened my agitation. So I delayed him as long as I could, asking for more and more things that would keep him around the house, like making another pot of coffee and fixing me breakfast (something he does joyfully and often!).

As he was making the second pot of coffee, I received a notification: my brother had died by suicide. I howled and wept and tried to articulate the news to my intimate partner. He immediately rushed over, held me in my sorrow, and said, "Now I understand why you didn't want me to leave this morning." In the weeks that followed, as I waded through the grief of the loss, I became increasingly grateful for my intuition and further understood its importance — *particularly when it is not yet understandable.*

Intuition does not always arise as a *result* of something. It may simply arise. Like a beacon from beyond, a message from our foremothers: *Listen.*

Hindsight is often 20/20. We can all look back at times in our lives when we *knew* something wasn't right and brushed it off or overlooked it...and regretted it. Maybe we had the sneaking hunch our intimate partner was lying to us, but we explained away the aberrant behavior. Maybe we felt sensations in our body that signaled ill health, but we masked it with a coping mechanism. Maybe we heard the cry of help or distress from our child, who was being bullied, and reasoned that all kids go through this and it's a normal stage of growing up.

Whenever we fail to honor our intuition and speak up about our unease, matters go unresolved — or worse. I am certain that every woman who reads this book knows this to the core of her being.

The only solution is to become comfortable with our unease. It's a precursor to making things good and right again! And while it certainly feels destabilizing or uncomfortable, accepting our unease is actually the seed that breeds life energy and further joy. We women, as preservers of the life force, are the first to feel it falter. That unease in our body is a signal to immediately course correct whatever is going on in our surroundings. It is ultimately a good thing. Though it may cause us and those around us some initial discomfort, that is well worth it in light of the alternative, which is watching things slide downhill.

Imagine if we spoke up about our unease the *first* time our partner lied to us and were honored and cherished enough to be heard. Consider the outcome of making a doctor's appointment at the *first* sign of physical distress, and even if we find out nothing is wrong, we alleviate that worry right away rather than carrying it with us for weeks or months. What if we overcame the initial tension of confronting a school authority about a child's bully immediately, rather than letting the suffering fester throughout the school year?

No doubt you can think of plenty of times in your life when the unease of your intuitive warning system would have benefited you had you spoken up or changed course immediately. The feminine is governed by time, and we have none to lose. We cannot procrastinate or postpone our unease for the (seeming) benefit of others' comfort. We cannot afford to sit meekly by, afraid to unleash our agency and get the matter addressed.

If we do, things only get worse.

This isn't a threat or a cautionary tale. This is a fact of life. Amazingly, we have the internal guidance system to alleviate a lot of our own suffering (and, by proxy, the suffering of those around us!). So consider the unease that arises from your feminine intuition to be your ultimate grace. The benevolent benediction built within you and guiding you toward a life of joy, health, peace, harmony, and love. Your feminine intuition serves you well, and by whatever means it signals you, it is showing you the pathway forward to your greatest satisfaction.

The Formula for Balance

When we own our intuitive feelings as the underlying drivers of satisfaction, then it becomes a no-brainer that we should heed them. I think of *Star Wars*' Princess Leia in this regard. She was one of my few childhood heroes who was a woman. She holds the title of princess, but we all know her to be a queen: one who is dignified and secure in her own mind, heart, body…and femininity.

Though small in stature, the actor Carrie Fisher played Princess Leia in a larger-than-life way as a powerful, confident woman. Leia is often the only female in the presence of men, and she never suffers scoundrels. Regardless of her entirely male surroundings, she directs the battle against the Empire (read: the patriarchy), and in what is perhaps the most intuitive moment of the original trilogy, she uses her Force-inspired intuition to turn the *Millennium Falcon* back toward danger — toward Darth Vader and his Imperial troops — as she follows an inner knowing that her brother, Luke Skywalker, must be saved.

Her quick command of "We have to go back" is met with some initial resistance from Lando Calrissian, who balks that the fighters are coming after them, but the animal-like Chewbacca (representing the force of nature) immediately sees the importance of Princess Leia's instructions. Without question, he veers from the course, turns the ship around, and saves Luke. It is a remarkable moment in movie history! And while Leia offers governance and insights to all the men around her, their cherishing of her title and the hope she provides for the rebellion lead them to honor her intuitive guidance unfailingly.

I wish this for us all. I wish for us all to be Princess Leias — no, Queen Leias! — in our own lives.

We are the tenders of life, the harbingers of life energy, and the purveyors of pleasure. When these things are cherished by the masculine, then intuitive guidance from the feminine is both heeded and *welcomed*. While this may seem like a lofty notion in your life right now, *it is possible* to cultivate a culture and community around you that honors your intuitive gifts and values your healthy expression of emotions.

When we are fully in the feminine, we are ready to receive this cherishing. I present it this way, because I see many women *chasing after* what they need in their lives. They pursue the intimate partner of their choice, they go after the career path, they hunt down their dreams, they give themselves away to their family and friends — all of which puts them fully in the masculine energy! The Satisfied Woman, on the other hand, stands firmly in her receptivity, and because she is the queen of herself, she remains confident and steadfast in her needs and desires...until the healthy masculine around her responds by actively contributing to and protecting those needs and desires.

I don't just mean this in terms of romantic partnerships, either. In any situation where you are most comfortable leaning fully into your fierce feminine essence, then remain steadfast and confident in that. May this be the unbreakable boundary that we set for ourselves moving forward.

It is through our femininity that we wield the most power. Remember, not power *over*, but power *with*. In this pursuit, our greatest allies are other confidently feminine women. These bonds of friendship and camaraderie foster power and give us the strength to pursue what is for the benefit of all. The strength of the feminine is that it empowers all and infuses every situation with life energy. When we feel drained of this life energy as a solution is being reached, we know that our femininity has been breached. Even though a resolution may require very hard or challenging steps, the more we check in with our intuitive guidance, the more we know if we are on the right path. As soon as we feel negativity arise, it's a signal that the path may need another course correction.

Remember, our masculine counterparts (and the culture we live in) prefer linear pathways to solutions. We must keep encouraging through our receptivity, fierce femininity, and intuitive knowing whichever pathway gets us to the best resolution...even if it periodically follows a circuitous route or becomes derailed.

This is why the ability to trust your environment and those around you (including your fellow feminine friends) is one of the Four Keys of femininity. Resolutions are not possible without trust. If we don't trust the masculine to cherish our emotions and intuition, it becomes a nonstarter when we need to draw attention to our unease. We (or they) diminish it, downplay it, or cast it aside. But we know how this works out ultimately, don't we? That nagging voice on the inside only grows louder when it is not heeded.

So we must cultivate the Four Keys in our lives, beginning with those who hold our first key — trust. This way, we can navigate any course corrections necessary when our sense of satisfaction feels compromised in any way.

In short, here's the ideal process:

Feminine: Remains steady and receptive in her feminine needs and intuitive guidance.

Masculine: Responds by cherishing her with protection and providership, asking, "How can I contribute to your safety, security, or sense of trust?"

Feminine: Vulnerably and honestly shares her feelings and intuition about the situation or condition at hand.

Masculine: Offers suggestions, solutions, and leadership toward resolution.

Feminine: May offer more feeling or insights in order to get the masculine on the right track to the most beneficial solution for all. She then receives the direction and leadership of the masculine and lets him do the work to resolve the issue while, with her feelings, she remains the barometer for how the work is going.

Keep in mind that this is a delicate process. It requires both feminine and masculine to be in an openhearted state of grace and tenderness. At no point in this process is power, control, criticism, or unkindness allowed. The masculine should watch for the tendency to manhandle the situation or gaslight the feminine into thinking that "everything is fine." The feminine needs to watch out for either sharp or harsh words ("You're doing it the wrong way!") or a passive subjugation of needs ("It's fine, just do what you want"). All parties must stand in their own feminine or masculine power and remain generous and kind until a resolution is reached.

Make no mistake, though. The resolution will *feel good* to the feminine and *be good* for all.

4

Making Meaning on Our Own Terms

The psyche is a complex landscape with many different features to explore and understand. What we are most familiar with is our conscious mind: the thoughts, feelings, hopes, and dreams that we are aware of at any given moment and that we show the world as our personality and through our interactions. It is with the conscious mind that we engage in conversation and rationally work through problems. It is also with the conscious mind that we take part in certain spiritual and psychological practices, like meditation, critical thinking, and various forms of talk therapy.

Of course, there is much more to us than the conscious mind.

Underneath it is the unconscious mind, which includes all that we are not aware of until the conscious brings it forth. Within our unconscious are all our deepest desires, wishes, and hopes, the things we see in our nightly dreamscapes and feel when we experience the synchronicities of life — like repeatedly seeing the symbol of a bird as a reminder of a loved one. The unconscious also harbors all our feelings, emotions, triggers, traumas, and our shadow — that which we do not wish to own and so repress. These are the things that respond to the hydraulic nature of the unconscious and pop up at the most inopportune times. Additionally, within the unconscious are the archetypes that populate our psyche and present as our reality.

A lot has been made of archetypes since the famed Swiss psychologist Carl Jung first coined the term to codify innate energies within the psyche. According to Jung, archetypes provide structure to the unconscious framework so that we can make sense of and understand more completely what is alive within us.

Even though there are an endless number of archetypes that manifest in our external lives, these days much effort is made to pigeonhole the psyche into ordered lists of archetypes.

A truly masculine thing to do.

What is true for the psyche is that it is endless. And boundless. While, as humans, we definitely have common threads and structures (which make psychology and the study thereof possible!), each of us is unique — especially in the way we draw forth and bring to life an archetype that is active in our psyche.

The short version is, many people have common archetypes within them, like the warrior, the sage, or the hero. But to try to create lists for the psyche to structure itself around is like trying to place the square key into the round hole. What's worse is attempting to embody or embrace the list and force the archetype to come forward on the basis of someone's write-up of it.

This isn't the spirit of archetypes at all. Rather, we must reverse engineer our own list by examining what is alive and true for us. We can look at our life, see what is present, and understand it better by analyzing the archetypes underneath it.

Archetypes are like the scaffolding of a building. There is no way to tell what the final design and features of an edifice will be by looking at the bare steel structure that will support it. However, once the building is complete, it's much easier to look with X-ray vision and understand how it is being held up.

For example, one common archetype for all humans is the hero, because we all grow up with stories of mythical heroes! Whether our heroes are super or mundane, historical or fictional, hero as archetype lives within our psyche. The way in which we discover our heroes outside of us helps us bring greater understanding to how they are structured for us on the inside.

Our personal archetype of hero has less to do with the kinds of heroes we find across all myths and more to do with the specific ones we resonate with or gravitate toward. The way we perceive the hero, how we talk about them, the heroic experiences we hold on to as adults — that all helps shape what we think we know and understand about the hero. Once we have an archetype that feels resonant, we can look to various structures — that is, examples — to help us understand it better.

This gets to the heart of Joseph Campbell's famous question: What myth do we live by? As we discover the myths and heroes that are most resonant to us, we gain a greater understanding of our internal archetypes and the stories and belief systems playing out in our life.

For example, if our concept of hero is something like Wonder Woman, then the archetype of Diana of the Amazons is helpful in contextualizing those qualities and providing structure for its valuable lessons. (We can be courageous *and* loving!) It gives us a framework for where to begin our own healing pathway around hero, whether we want to embody it more in our lives, resolve our past relationships or anything that pulls us out of a heroic state, or simply understand the varied richness of hero expressed in the world around us.

This is merely one example, and for all women reading this book, you know how challenging it is to find feminine heroes illuminated in modern mythology! In fact, I present the ready image of Wonder Woman because it is a character that was redone so brilliantly in recent memory that it inspired a mild breakdown for me. After seeing the Gal Gadot film in the movie theater, I reached my vehicle in heaving sobs and sat there for twenty minutes before I realized why it was so impactful: I didn't have many heroes like Diana Prince growing up. Neither did many other women, as countless female viewers found themselves deeply touched by Gadot's portrayal of this feminine hero.

Aside from Wonder Woman, and perhaps the 1980s cartoon She-Ra, heart-based feminine warriors are few and far between in our culture. Typically, women in myth are presented as the damsel in distress, the subservient sidekick, or in a negative light as the black widow poised to poison the masculine in her midst. (Praise to Marvel Comics for redefining the Black Widow as a positive feminine hero!)

If archetypes are meant to provide understandable, externalized frameworks of what is alive within us, then what, as women, are we to work with? If you have ever looked into the archetypes traditionally ascribed to women, you know they go like this:

> **Maiden:** Virginal and pure (ages approximately ten to twenty-five)
>
> **Lover:** Pleasure filled and pleasure driven (ages approximately twenty-five to forty)
>
> **Mother:** Nurturing and generative (ages approximately forty to fifty-five)
>
> **Crone:** Wise and cunning (ages approximately fifty-five and beyond)

No surprises there. These classic archetypes oversimplify the life stages of a woman and relegate the feminine psyche either to her attractiveness to men (maiden, lover), or her usefulness to men (mother, crone). But as we all know, there is far more to the tapestry of the feminine unconscious than what she is capable of in relationship to men and those in her care.

If we look at more modern compilations of common archetypes — supposedly neutral ones — we still find lists that are predominantly driven by the masculine paradigm: ruler, magician, sage, explorer, rebel, everyman…While it is certainly true that women can be any of these, such roles hold a great deal more mythology for men.

It's time for us to dig into the feminine psyche and imagine our way to new, uncharted archetypal realities. If the magician typically exists in our psyche as male, how can we redefine and elevate a great mage like the Lady of the Lake, untangling her from her role solely in relationship to Arthur and Excalibur, his magical sword (read: penis), in the tales of Avalon? If the classic midcentury male movie heartthrob is Cary Grant, how can we revise our history so that we view Marilyn Monroe, not as a tragic character whose only virtue was her exceptional figure, but rather as a brilliant actor who wielded her feminine power to leave a stunning film legacy?

We can find a solution by examining the process of psychological transformation and the steps the psyche must undertake to reach its pinnacle, whether that be called maturity, individuation, or enlightenment. Various thinkers like Sigmund Freud, Carl Jung, and Joseph Campbell have given us their interpretation of the development of the human psyche...but all from a masculine perspective, of course. We need only look to the great goddess archetypes offered to us throughout history — those who have maintained their wildness and resisted domination or manipulation by masculine forces — to find inspiration for how the feminine psyche evolves to her pinnacle: by ascending to the throne of the queen. Even that idea of pinnacle elicits a peak, a projectile, a (dare I say?) penile force. For women, the development of our psyches is cyclical, with a zenith *and* a nadir. And, of course, we can make a strong psychological case for understanding the depths of the psyche to be the particular domain of the feminine, with its creative unconscious, its mythical pathways of dreams, and its wild and unpredictable landscape of emotions and intuition. The feminine is the province of birth *and* rebirth, of creating something from (almost) nothing. So perhaps instead of thinking of feminine psychological transformation as reaching a peak, let's consider it instead as reaching a climax...over and over again (wink, wink).

If we look to the great goddess of Egypt, Isis, we see her

proudly owning all that is most feminine on her climactic throne as the queen. She is the protector of death and the mother of the celestial falcon god, Horus. She is the bringer and reviver of life, having reconfigured her brother and husband, Osiris, after a terrible dismemberment and resurrecting him...while also crafting him a new penis! She is commonly depicted sitting on a throne as she presides over all, above and below ground, with grand wings spread to either side in an all-encompassing embrace, wearing a headdress in the shape of the Egyptian hieroglyph for *throne*. She is the daughter of the earth and sky and possesses mystical powers, which is why historically she had orders of priestesses trained in her intuitive gifts and spiritual practices. She initiates us into girlhood, womanhood, motherhood, and mavenhood, protecting each cycle of a woman's life.

Rather than labeling these classic stages in terms of their function in relationship to men, let's take inspiration from Isis herself and rethink them in women's terms, according to the intrinsic values each of the stages embraces:

- **Inception:** Our entry into and exploration of who we can be as a woman (ages approximately ten to twenty-five)
- **Sensation:** The experience and choice of who we are as a woman (ages approximately twenty-five to forty)
- **Initiation:** The ownership and integration of our fullest expression of womanhood (ages approximately forty to fifty-five)
- **Satisfaction:** The utilization of the fruits of our initiation to serve as inspiration and guide to others (ages approximately fifty-five and beyond)

Perhaps the most unique thing about the feminine psyche is that it is biologically dominated by the cyclical hormonal realities that dictate her life. This is something that biological men do not have to contend with, and so they are able to manifest nearly any reality they choose at any time past puberty. Young men can become fathers. Older men can remain puerile (as in the Peter Pan syndrome). A man's career can last his entire lifetime. And as a society we value this freewheeling, time-defying ability to choose who we wish to be at any time we wish to be it.

But this is not the case for women. We cannot become mothers at any age. Our career may be derailed by the biological act of childbearing. Older women's bodies change in ways that challenge the kind of youthfulness that men seem to retain. (If we recall the Peter Pan story, we remember that it was only boys who were lost and never grew up, while Wendy's fate was quite different.) Of course, men have different struggles throughout their lives and different challenges laid on them by the culture.

And that's the point.

Men's struggles *are* different. And yet, somehow, as women in female bodies who embrace the feminine, we're still expected to live by male standards. We even expect it of ourselves. During our fertile years, the lengths we go to to hide the effects of our monthly menstrual cycles and the ways they affect our psyche, emotions, and energy levels (lest our ire be dismissed simply as PMS — as if *that* were not a real phenomenon — by our male counterparts). Young women choose a career path and put off the motherhood we desire long past the time our bodies are capable of healthy pregnancy. As we age, women are taking more and more extreme measures to preserve the youthful appearance of our bodies and faces. In the meantime, our grandmothers are hidden away in retirement homes, with infrequent visits from family.

If we are to fully embrace our physical womanhood and our inherent femininity, then we need to lean into the cycles of our life that are at the heart of what makes us women and understand the *different and cyclical nature of our psyche* that allows us to thrive. We are privileged to have an underlying biological structure that ensures we live a full and complete life. We *must* live through the monthly cycles of menstruation and face the blood and mess that make us women without sanitizing them or glossing them over. We *must* live through fecund years with the responsibility of potential motherhood, whether or not we choose to have children. We *must* live through the biological changes of menopause and readjust to being a wise woman and mentor to others. And when society tries to force us to ignore our cyclical nature because *they* don't want to see the reality, it creates a schism and a shame inside of us that contribute to the denial of our feminine gifts.

I remember this experience from my youth, when I first started menstruating. It was a traumatic experience because my anatomy is not compatible with tampons. When I tried using them, the blood slid right by and onto my jeans or down my legs in front of classmates who ridiculed me and cowed me into fearing my own body's natural processes. Rather than celebrating this biological rite into womanhood, I was terrified and ashamed of what my body was doing to me. It was psychologically devastating. And the remedy presented to me was not to empower my young self around the monthly event. Rather, the "solution" was to get birth control shots in the arm that removed my monthly cycle altogether, altering my young hormonal balance.

It wasn't until much later in life — my early thirties, really — that I realized the dishonor I experienced by repressing my body's gifts and the depression that arose from the denial of my womanhood. I tell this story because I know I'm not alone. It has become more and more commonplace for women to hide, deny, repress, medicate, and alter the biological foundations of femininity. This is not to vilify all the amazing advances in medicine and technology that keep us healthy and provide us with freedom of choice regarding reproduction, but rather to point out the *additional* ways those methods are used to perpetuate the alteration and repression of femininity. I want women to have freedom of choice — to be able to choose to be women of agency *and* to lean into their fullest feminine expression.

With that in mind, let's explore the biological foundations of femininity and how our female body's unique life cycles can give rise to the fullest expression of satisfaction as women.

The Inception Phase: Exploration

All children under about the age of ten are rooted in the feminine polarity. They require protection, cherishing, nurturing, structure, and leadership, and they must be provided for. They are inquisitive by nature, questioning every inch of their surroundings, and exist in playful creativity with active imaginations. Psychologically, around the ages of nine to twelve, they begin to individuate into their own polarities. We notice this as the time when children stop playing easily in mixed-gendered groups and start developing more gender-based cliques and interests, with differences in types of play and self-expression. Biologically speaking, it is also around this time that puberty begins and hormones infiltrate the brains of young people. Those hormones are powerful, helping form the basis of the feminine or masculine psyche.

The *inception phase* starts around age ten. For the young girl, it is around this time that menstruation begins. This is the undeniable demarcation of womanhood. It means that she inhabits a body that is now capable of producing life. This is not only a momentous change; it is a tremendous responsibility. This biological process represents a psychological thrust into a new phase of life: childhood is left behind, and she must face a new reality. It is an unceremonious coming of age that nature delivers, whether the young girl is psychologically prepared for it or not. Because of the biological process, the young girl's psyche *must* process her new reality, and she *must* come to grips with this truth — and continue to face it every single month.

Rites of passage into adulthood are a part of most every mythological and religious tradition historically and worldwide. While they exist for both young men and women, they are far more common, pronounced, and important for young men. Why? Because the journey into biological adulthood for men is a slow burn they might miss. Without a coming-of-age ritual or traumatic event (for example, the loss of a father, which may cause the young boy to now be the "man of the house"), the young male psyche may fail to see the less pronounced or unorganized societal or familial cues. The work of scholars like the cultural mythologist Kwame Scruggs and his Alchemy Inc. organization addresses this uniquely male issue by providing young men with the structures and rituals their psyches need to graduate from childhood into adulthood.

For a young girl? The sudden, undeniable biological event of menstruation incites a reckoning the psyche cannot ignore. She is now a woman — full stop. Her psyche may need to develop further to adjust to the realities of her physical truth, but her physical truth cannot be hidden, quashed, or denied for very long. Unfortunately, being a young girl these days still comes with a host of expectations left over from the patriarchal ideals infused into this society. With the initial primal archetype of the maiden comes, first and foremost, the expectation of her being quiet and virginal. A "good girl" who smiles often and doesn't call attention to herself beyond being the apple of her family's eye.

As soon as a young woman individuates beyond the meek and mild expectations of society and becomes her own woman, perhaps exerting her opinions or dressing less like a child, the repercussions begin. As she passes her tween years, the drive to dress and act like a grown woman creates a tension between premature sexualization and the freedom to grow and develop without the pressure of being sexually attractive. The battle between the wills of the young woman and her caregivers or authority figures shapes who she becomes and impacts whether or not she decides to don masculine armor to brave the masculine world of her upbringing.

But what if there were a different path for the young lady? What if, until about twenty-five years of age or so, she was taught to revere her womanhood and lean into her femininity?

What if we were to give young women the permission necessary to be confidently feminine? What if we offered them structure and support around the changes in their bodies, normalizing the occasional bleed through the pants and the awkward eruption of breasts? What if we let young women discover their feminine gifts of intuition and emotions rather than punishing them for being irrational teenagers? As these young girls move out into the world on their own, finding their footing as young women and, eventually, full-fledged adults, what if we ensured safe passage and non-discrimination so they could walk freely at night down whatever street they chose?

Or, as in the myth of Persephone, what if we allowed her to pick the flowers she desires and live in the world of her own making? This original Greek myth is often told in such a way that it takes the point of view of the mother, Demeter, chastising Persephone for her naive choice of flower and blaming her for her own abduction by Hades. Demeter tries to keep Persephone virginal and innocent, restricting her interactions with others so that she stays in her mother's control. Well, young girls like Persephone possess the powers of intuition and emotion, and Persephone's intuition is strong enough to lead her to an enchanting meadow where the god of the underworld, Hades, pulls her down into his homeland when she plucks a narcissus flower. (We can't overlook the symbology of the flower as headstrong Persephone chooses herself with the petals!) From Demeter's point of view, this "abduction" is a tragedy and causes her, the goddess of the harvest, to restrict the earth's growing period to the time of year, spring and summer, when Persephone leaves the underworld to come visit her.

What if, from Persephone's point of view, this incredible act of inquiry and choice brings her closer to her desires and intuition? What if with Hades in his underworld is where Persephone most longs to be? What if that metaphorical *nekyia* — the place in our unconscious that harbors our dreams and emotions — is Persephone's perfect domain? We often remove both inquisition and agency from young girls, thinking we know best, when in fact it is sometimes their brazen choices that open up whole new worlds for them to explore and inhabit.

In the past, the archetypal understanding of the maiden was so sanitized and restricted, it didn't allow for the full expression of the feminine but, rather, only what the patriarchy and distorted masculine *allowed*. The patriarchy can't handle young females' sexuality or their desire to be strong and powerful — or strongly emotional and powerfully intuitive. There is a growing acceptance of and encouragement for young women to use their intelligence (for example, in female-oriented initiatives in STEM education), as well as some advancements in sports (though we still have a long way to go there). But to leave out support for the elements that make young girls' feminine psyches thrive means we're not helping them find the fullness of their expression as feminine women.

Remember, it isn't *what* a woman does that makes her feminine. It is *how* she does it. The young lady, during the inception phase, can lean into her smarts as long as all her inquisitiveness is honored and valued as a core element. She can choose to play fiercely on the soccer field as long as the emotional upset of defeat is loved and supported. Let her be who she is and *let her be on her way to becoming a Satisfied Woman*. This is the incept inducting herself into her world, using her burgeoning intuitive gifts to assess her life, embrace her talents, discover her joy, and take her initial steps toward satisfaction. This is when the young woman explores *who she can ultimately be as the Satisfied Woman*.

The Sensation Phase: Experiences and Choice

It is not exact timing, and it's not as if we receive it on our birthday wrapped with a bow, but around age twenty-five, the brain reaches its final stage of development. The last piece of the puzzle is the prefrontal cortex, which gives us the ability to integrate emotions with logic. For our purposes, this means our ability to navigate both polarities within: the masculine and the feminine. We are capable of having appropriately calibrated emotional responses, which is a progression from our younger years, when small events had major emotional consequences and our rational thinking had not yet reached a level of mastery. Think of the devastation of teenage breakups or the seemingly critical choice of the right outfit to suit the day. By around age twenty-five, we have enough life experience to prioritize things more clearly than before and also to understand the consequences of behavior more fully.

While a breakup or bad test score may once have felt like a small death, the more fully developed brain understands that these trials are part of life and that we will be faced with bigger choices that will have greater consequences. Even so, the young woman, beginning around her midtwenties, has an extraordinary opportunity. This is her time to make important choices boldly and from her heart and let them shape who she is. While for the young incept, the world is her oyster and choices be damned, when we reach the developmental stage of the sensate, things become not only more clear but more consequential.

Cyndi Lauper was, of course, right about the fact that girls just wanna have fun, and the revolutionary development of the birth control pill gave women a sexual freedom they never had prior to 1960 (a mere three generations ago!). There are greater and more unique challenges for a woman born in a man's world than there are for men. We have the pressure of our biology dictating the flow of our lives to some extent, and we also still find ourselves at a disadvantage in many areas of life. (Women still only earn eighty cents to every dollar a man earns, for example.) In this initial stage of adulthood, the consequences of our intimate actions are more serious and far-reaching than they would be for a man. For example, an unwanted pregnancy at this age typically results in prolonged periods of anxiety and stress, while an abortion has lasting psychological consequences. Women bear the brunt of the reproductive choices of all.

This period of a woman's life is a time to solidify who she is, how she expresses herself, and what she wants to receive from the world. The dominant narrative of our culture emphasizes a confusing conflagration of messages, though. It says that the young lady in her twenties and thirties needs to use this time to become independent, pursue a career, be her own woman... *and* find a relationship *and* consider whether she wants to start a family. This is the "Women must be all things all the time to all people" messaging that leads to women donning the mask of masculinity and then feeling burned out and overwhelmed. Without the support she needs to drop that mask, it is very difficult for a woman to find the time and space to settle into the fullness of her feminine expression.

This has complicated consequences. While, on the one hand, the pursuit of career and calling creates a sense of fulfillment, it can cause one's feminine aspects to harden and the masculine polarity to overcompensate. And while things at work might be going great — promotions, rewarding career choices, exciting opportunities — dating and personal relationships may be complicated, inauthentic, or nonexistent as a result. Basically, with the pursuit of traditional forms of masculine success during this period of our lives, we sacrifice this precious time to hone our internal feminine gifts of intuition, creativity, receptivity, and emotional connection to ourselves and maybe even to those we love or could fall in love with.

Think of the Roman myth of the great huntress Diana. Her symbology is a perfect parallel to this stage of a woman's life. She aligns herself with the moon and its phases, just as a menstruating woman must. She is governed by her nature, as represented by her alliance with all the creatures of the forest. And she is revered as an incredible huntress, her chosen career path! Perhaps the most enlivening part of Diana's story is her fierce protection of and governance over her own body. While bathing, she is spied on by Actaeon. In reaction to his inappropriately prying eyes, she transforms him into a deer to be hunted by his own hounds. Diana suffers no distortion of the masculine, and she readily calls upon her wild intuition (the animals who protect her) and fierce hunting skills to ensure she always reinforces her own feminine needs and desires.

I don't doubt that you know women in this stage of their lives who have kicked proverbial ass and forged career pathways none before them have, but who have trouble on the dating scene and also have extraordinary difficulty asking for support in getting their feminine needs met. I have watched countless women do the work hustle for a decade or more, only to realize too late that they are running out of time to pursue that other common desire of adult womanhood: childbearing.

The choice to have children is a difficult topic to discuss, as it is intertwined with very strong opinions. Not all women are mothers. Not all women can be mothers. And not all women want to be mothers. For the traditional archetypal blueprint of a woman's life to include motherhood as a fait accompli reduces her value to the capacity to bear children — and devalues her if she doesn't. Statistically, around 80 percent of women today have children, leaving at least one out of five of your female friends (or yourself) in the childless category. Whether by choice or by biology, that means that many women are finding different creative outlets outside of procreativity.

This wasn't always an available choice. While a woman's biology and health have always played a role in her ability to conceive, it is a very recent cultural evolution that women can simply opt out of motherhood if they so choose. Many women have been subject to the societal, religious, or political narratives of the past and not had that choice. My grandmother was one among them. She was raised in a complicated time in prewar Eastern Europe, long before readily available, safe contraception. She had five pregnancies, three miscarriages, and, ultimately, two daughters. In her confessional period later in life, she confided to me once in the kitchen over cookies that she enjoyed her career so much (she worked at a sugar company as the copyist before Xerox machines were invented) that she would have preferred not to have had children.

Of course, I'm grateful that she did, so that I have the opportunity to be here to emphasize for my readers *the choices that she never had.* And while it is true that the majority of women desire motherhood as part of their lives, the fact is that today, *this is an option when it never was before.* These new opportunities that women are presented with highlight the second stage of life: the *sensation phase.*

While we have the choice to have children or not, what we don't have choice around is the timing of this experience. Again, because we inhabit a woman's biological body, we are entirely subject to the rules of its biological clock. And while advances in science and medicine have stretched that timeline to some extent, providing opportunities for pregnancy that would have been unimaginable even a few decades ago, there are still limits. As much as we don't want this to be the case and as unfair as it is, we cannot argue with our body's reality. Even though it is said that a woman's prerogative is to change her mind, our choices (especially about this point) are governed by biology and time.

A clear choice must be made. And the timing of it coincides with this period of the sensation. Because this time is not only about exploring our world through career and external relationships, it is about deciding who we are as our feminine selves and exerting agency over our choices to ensure our greatest feminine expression — whether or not that includes having a family. There are many ways to express creativity without being procreative! The bearing of children, while the exclusive province of those born with a womb, is only one of the many facets of womanhood. We have options for how to manifest our femininity, but we need to choose clearly what brings the most satisfaction and joy to our life at this time. It may be the pursuit of a career. It may be experiencing avenues of passion and creativity. It may be starting a family and entering parenthood.

While we hear a lot about the notion of a "work/life balance" in women's lives, having that is generally the privilege of someone in a position of power in their career, where they've earned the seniority to be able to call the shots around when they work and how much work they take home. Even for entrepreneurs, it's difficult to achieve life balance when they are building the business and must use every ounce of the hustle they have to get it off the ground. Not to mention the very real impact of pregnancy discrimination in the workplace and the fact that every major corporation has statistics on how much productivity is lost due to pregnancy and pregnancy leave, which is not something corporations favor. (No, this is not fair, but it is still the patriarchal world we live in today.) It would be amazing for the workplace to support and *reward* parenthood and create an equal playing field in that regard!

Even though the current social narrative is that "women can do it all," we need to respond with thoughtful inquiry — questions like "*Should* we do it all?" and "Do we actually *want* to do it all?" Trying to focus 100 percent of our energy on forging ahead in a kick-ass career path *and* putting 100 percent of our efforts into parenthood is a faulty equation. We only have 100 percent total to offer at any given time. But because of the patriarchal structures of corporations and the hierarchy of the individual workplace, offering only a 50 percent effort is a recipe for being overlooked and undervalued. Not to mention that being able to devote only 50 percent of our energy to parenthood is less than a child may need. Of course, any of these equations leave absolutely nothing for our own feminine needs and desires.

The most important question for the sensate is not "Can we do it all?" but, rather, "When do we want to do what?" As I said, it is all about timing.

So during our period as the sensate, we may need to turn topsy-turvy the societal expectations of the patriarchy. Depending on our early explorations and experiences of womanhood during the inception phase, we may decide that what is most important — nay, most satisfying — to us in our femininity is not the ardent pursuit of career, but instead the intuitive pursuit of creative endeavors. Or perhaps it becomes clear that having a family is the pathway of choice, in which case, a later stage of life may present the best time to endeavor to build a career. While it is *absolutely true* that women can do it all, we need to balance the delicate *timing* of our biology with our choices so that we satisfy all our desires. Men can start careers, have families, pursue passions at any age. Women, unfortunately, don't have that luxury. We can have it all, but we must decide *when* we want to have it.

Rather than try to retrofit our biology into the expectations appropriate to a man within a patriarchal world, only to end up disappointed and out of time when our body dictates the choices for us, let us honor who we are as women and use the period of the sensate to explore *who and what feel most satisfying to us*, whether that be our (pro)creative pursuits, intimate partnership, or the intuitive gifts that our feminine soul holds. It is by honing these intuitive gifts in this phase that we are best able to choose what will make us the Satisfied Woman.

A Note about Choice

The sensation phase is defined by choice: the ability to explore our world as feminine women and pick what is right for us in the right time. This, of course, assumes that all choices are possible. When I write about the sensation phase of our lives in this way, I write about it as an ideal. And for those women lucky enough to be able to exercise every choice they want, I thank our lucky stars that we live in this time when that is possible for some. That said, many choices are denied to us as women or have been taken away. We are even still fighting for full control of our bodies and reproductive rights. Our personal geography, ethnicity, socioeconomic status, and/or cultural condition may limit some of the choices we are able to make.

While I recognize and understand that not all choices may be available to you, I write this in the hopes that they are. Books are timeless, and though this book hits shelves at a certain moment in history, it will last far longer (I hope!). My sincere wish is that I write this book for all the choices you have to make now *and* for all the choices that women reading this in the future are able to make. May our every choice empower the next woman to be able to make even more choices of her own.

Rethinking Motherhood

I've already mentioned that every child up until about the age of ten — when emotional development and early stages of puberty begin — is in the feminine polarity. Children need to be cherished and nurtured, to be kept safe and secure, and to have great trust in the world around them. They are relentlessly inquisitive and endlessly creative. These qualities are so revered in children that we often try to recapture them as adults.

This does present an interesting conundrum, though. When children under ten are in the household inhabiting the feminine polarity, those in caretaking roles must all fall into the masculine polarity to support, guide, nurture, and protect them. Including us.

This means that for even the fiercest feminine woman, there is a period of about ten child-rearing years when she needs to down-shift her own feminine essence in favor of the masculine traits required to get children to their next stage of life. While the act of *becoming* pregnant and *being* pregnant are exclusively in the feminine domain (it would be hard to deny the creativity in pro-creation!), at the moment of birth, you are thrust into parenthood, which is its own exclusively masculine expression of life.

It seems counterintuitive to think that parenthood is a masculine endeavor, especially since children are born of women's bodies. But remember that all humans have both polarities within them, and because of the special feminine status of young humans under ten, it simply means that one of the great acts of love in parenthood is that we bring our masculinity to the forefront to protect, guide, nurture, and provide for them. And if you are a single mother, your task is even greater in this capacity.

No one said child-rearing was easy. Most parents tell you it is the hardest (but most rewarding) thing they will ever do. However, it is important to go into those formative years of child-rearing with eyes open and your feminine resources well fortified, because you will leave your feminine polarity behind for a decade or so while your life energy is devoted to your young. This has a big impact on intimate relationships, as now both parties are thrust into the masculine on behalf of the kids. In intimate relationships where you are the feminine counterpart, this can be particularly jarring. What once was a balanced relationship between the two of you now shifts into a balance between the two of you and the child.

For the feminine woman in this partnership, motherhood imparts many gifts and skyrockets the quality of nurturing that is a hallmark of this period. The nurturing element of parenthood is shared by both caregivers, regardless of primary polarity, but it is fundamentally a masculine trait. Nurturing is the foremost quality of a *parent*, not specifically of a woman. When you consider the definition of *nurturing*, which is to encourage growth and development, it is easy to understand that this actually falls under the masculine domain. Only because women have been culturally designated as the primary caregivers is this quality generally thought to be a female's domain and the reason why we see so many women inhabiting careers based in nurturing: education, health care, social work. And while nurturing is a human quality, many women take it on and lean into it more fully as a result of parenthood (or similar caregiving pursuits they explore throughout life). Men, on the other hand, are often misunderstood as not capable of nurturing, even though it is a profoundly masculine quality.

As parents settle into child-rearing in the masculine polarity, along with the joy and delight of nurturing a young life, struggles often arise due to the full-time nature of this role. While many women slide easily into the more masculine role of child-rearing, it may also make them feel drained of life force, overwhelmed, and even resentful of their partner and family for all the demands now placed on them. Parents have the tough job of providing what the family needs during this time, and so it is important that there be no mistaking that masculinity is required from caregivers. As crucially, partners and other support persons must give the feminine woman some slack and understanding for having to occupy a polarity that is not her own for a while.

Otherwise, the masculine partner feels as if he's lost his feminine partner. He may feel this when the mother prioritizes the children's needs over the father's. The mother may take on an executive role in the household, making decisions and governing schedules, and subsequently intimacy wanes. This scenario, of course, is not without its inherent difficulties, but it can be managed when intimate partners go in with open eyes and a clear understanding that they choose to undertake a decade of child-rearing together, for the well-being of the entire family. It is even a good idea to make agreements or arrangements for how to allow opposing polarities to reemerge once the child has reached ten or so years of age.

To complicate matters, modern culture holds a viewpoint that once a parent, always a parent. That somehow children require us not just to give of ourselves, but to give up ourselves. This is where coming-of-age rituals are incredibly handy. The function of these rituals is both to push the child into adulthood and also to start to release the caregivers from the responsibility of parenthood and give them back to themselves. Coming-of-age rituals have been practiced throughout the duration of human culture and are a part of every religious and spiritual tradition around the world. The human psyche possesses an inner knowing that a marked shift — an event, a commencement — must take place around the onset of puberty for the child to become an adult who will be responsible for him- or herself.

Of course, any parent will tell you, "But they'll always be my kids!" I get it. My mother still sends me holiday gifts wrapped up with bows, like the ones she used to give me when I was little. There is always a part of us that retains the parental quality. But truly healthy psychological growth for both puberty-age children and adults allows for the child to witness the adult as they are, in their own polarity, in their own relationship, in their own life, modeling personal responsibility and adulthood. That is as valuable a lesson as any!

It makes sense that kids still need support, guidance, and nurturing for many more years beyond this tender age, but their psychological development at that point has the capacity to understand parents as separate human beings, apart from them and with their own dynamic relationship. Their parents' autonomy and individual polarities foster independence in the young person, too, as they go out and explore their own dominant polarity in this very important phase of their young life.

The Initiation Phase: Integration

This archetypal phase of a woman's life is traditionally labeled "the mother," a title that implies a woman must first be "the lover" for all her fertile years until she conceives, and then she's locked into her role as "the mother." And that's it. In the eyes of the patriarchy, "lover" and "mother" are the foremost functions of women.

The patriarchy, of course, has it wrong.

As I've been saying throughout this chapter, women can do everything and be everything they want. They do and are those things in their own feminine way — with creativity, pleasure, life energy, receptivity, emotional drive, and intuitive guidance. The issue is not one of *can* we do something but *when* we do something. In terms of the biggest and perhaps most important choice of a woman's life, whether to undertake parenthood, the parenting stage takes a good ten years or so and lays itself over the sensation phase and perhaps also some of the initiation phase. Biologically speaking, the initiation phase begins around the age of forty, generally considered to be the point past which fertility declines. (Technically, peak fertility is in our twenties and begins to decline around age thirty-five.) By this point, we have likely made the choice to have children and have embarked on the parenthood phase...or not.

The point here is that even though this part of a woman's life is classically labeled as the time of "the mother," there is actually *so much more available* to women at this stage!

Even if we choose to have a child as late as our bodies can handle, we will still have years in the initiation phase that allow us to take ourselves back and settle fully into our womanhood. The most important and perhaps culturally controversial element here is the idea that women would relinquish the sole identity of mother for something — anything — else.

The repressive nature of the patriarchy does not want to give women the freedom to be themselves. As young women in the inception phase, we are viewed as the property of our families. (If you grew up with an overly protective caregiver who gave all your dates the third degree, you know what I'm talking about!) During the sensation phase, the societal pressure to achieve and succeed on masculine terms and be all things to everyone puts incredible pressure on the woman's wild, free, feminine nature to inhibit her experience of her world and curb her choice of what is right for her at the right time. When women become mothers, it is expected that they retain that role...forever. Or at least until that caretaking role shifts into that of a grandmother.

If we are to truly be free as women, in such a way that demonstrates to our daughters and other women what kind of personal freedom is possible, then we need to own each phase of our life accordingly and release the phases we have outgrown — or, perhaps more importantly in the case of the initiate, the phase that our children have outgrown.

If you're reading this and the idea of releasing the identity of mother feels terrifying, trust me that you are not alone. What might energize this idea and give it some life inside you is the question "What *else* am I if not just a mother?" If your individual feminine identity has been lost (to parenthood, career pursuits, or, really, anything else), then the initiation phase is your opportunity to reclaim it — to reclaim yourself.

The initiation phase represents the confident woman who is settled into how she defines and orients herself in her feminine polarity. We might say she has finally arrived! Home to herself, that is. The first phase of life, the inception, represents wide-eyed exploration and discovery. The second phase, the sensation, gives us our ability to feel and experience all the things that make us satisfied, so that we solidify them as part of our life moving forward. The initiation represents the intuitive knowing of ourselves as the Satisfied Woman. We now discern what makes us tick, tickled, and ticked off. What's most exciting is that the confident, clear, intuitive initiate is *comfortable*. Not complacent. But comfortable.

She derives comfort in who she is, no longer seeking after the approval of others — particularly men. She owns her intellect, her skill set, and, most importantly, her intuitively driven decisions. She is fully initiated into femininity. She claims it. At this point, she has spent the first half-ish of her life in a discovery mode, saddled with big choices very early. She has made those choices. She has had time to live with them. She knows which ones worked for her and which didn't. And now she's ready to be completely herself. Comfortable in her own skin.

One of the great qualities of the initiate is her practiced confidence in her intuition. She's likely been through plenty of circumstances in her past where she ignored it, second-guessed it, or let someone else talk her out of it. At this point, she's borne the brunt of those consequences and is no longer willing to suffer them. She is unafraid to speak up for herself and let her discomfort be heard. It is this confidence that actually helps her be *even more comfortable.* She has settled into her femininity and *knows* it is the essence of who she is. She is fully initiated into life as the feminine woman.

We tend to think of initiates as those just beginning on the path. While that may be one definition, for our purposes here an initiate is one who is inducted into a sisterhood because she has earned her place through a lifetime of trials, tribulations, and lived experience. She may still have things to learn about femininity and womanhood (we look to our elder satisfied sisters for those lessons), but she is fully in her power and essence as a feminine woman in the initiation phase.

Like the goddess Hathor of the Egyptian pantheon, the initiate protects other women and is in her fullness as a feminine woman ruling her place in the world. In Egypt, Hathor's temple in Dendera was the sacred home of the feminine mysteries. It's where legions of ladies gathered to perform rites that honored womanhood. Hathor is the protector of all women and all things sacred to women. She is the goddess of intimate love, sensuality, motherhood, beauty, dancing, music, and other arts. She is depicted with the horns of a cow, and so like Ariadne and the Minotaur, Hathor is no stranger to her internal nature, her wild and true emotions, and the trustworthiness of her intuition. In her temple, only women are allowed. This is her intimate circle of initiates, those who help her protect other women and their most important gift: their connection to their emotional intuition. She offers guidance and support to her sisterhood, but mostly she stands as a beacon of example to other women about the joys of empowered womanhood.

Hathor's feminine power, grace, connection to intuition, and commitment to her community are all hallmarks of the initiation phase. We understand that competition with other women was never necessary. Instead, we crave collaboration. We stand in our true nature and speak up clearly for our needs, knowing that when we do so, it helps pave the way for others around us to get their needs met, too. We are unapologetically feminine, even when it means our wild emotions come as a surprise or our inquiry derails prior assumptions.

And look, if you're in the initiation phase now and this description doesn't sound like you, then it's time to settle in. This can absolutely be you. This *is* you. All you need is to gather up your great history, take stock of the intuitive lessons you've learned (either by honoring your intuition or by passing it up), surround yourself with a heartfelt sisterhood, and recalibrate your life. It may be time for some housekeeping — no, *life keeping*. No one more than the initiate is prepared to get rid of what no longer serves her, whether it be an intimate partner, a career, friendships, habits, belief systems...you name it. If it doesn't have your highest good at heart or the Four Keys at its foundation, then, as my stepmother would say, "Get it gone."

This is your time to integrate all the lessons of the exploration phase of the incept and the choices made by the sensate through her experiences. The initiation phase is when you form a feminine foundation from all you have learned in your life so far. You reap the rewards of those efforts now, as you settle into satisfaction and lovingly but firmly reject all that creates discomfort in your heart, body, and soul.

The Satisfaction Phase: Discernment and Inspiration

During the summer of 2023, the movie *Barbie* took the world by storm. While I would love to congratulate director-cowriter Greta Gerwig on her astute mythologizing of the patriarchy and the female condition as well as write a whole dissertation on the finer points of the film, I leave you to watch it for yourself and bring to you this one fabulous line (of many) from the movie. Barbie escapes her plastic world and finds herself on a bus stop bench in LA, sitting next to a white-haired older woman. Barbie has never seen an older woman before, and in her shock and awe, she looks lovingly at her and says, "You're so beautiful." The radiant older woman confidently replies, "I know it!"

If only the whole world saw older women this way.

Society has historically seen women beyond the age of menopause as irrelevant, not of value, not sexy, not beautiful, and certainly not satisfied — that is, when it sees them at all. Our culture hides them away, retiring them from careers, pulling them off magazine covers, and replacing them with younger models. It is easy to surmise that because they no longer are believed to be sexually desirable to men and are past the age of procreation, the patriarchal culture has no use for postmenopausal women. And so they are relegated to the background, to fade into invisibility without so much as an afterthought.

When, in truth, this is perhaps when women have *the most* to offer the world. After a lifetime of her own satisfying struggles and glorious choices, *she has cultivated the incredible wisdom she now passes down to younger women.* Whether it be the epigenetic information her genomes pass down that becomes her granddaughter's intuition or the sage advice she offers to the younger women around her, the Satisfied Woman beyond the age of menopause could not be more valuable. She has the most power (and least f*cks to give) when it comes to calling the shots and defining the behavior of a new generation. Of course, classically a woman in this archetypal stage is called "the crone." Bleh. What woman *ever* wants to be thought of as a crone!

I remember as a child having a coloring book of fairy tales, and the crone appears in many: "Hansel and Gretel," "Rapunzel," "Cinderella." Inevitably, the crone is depicted as ugly, disagreeable, close to death, and the wielder of sinister magic. No one wants to befriend the crone. She is often incredibly dangerous to young people — especially young women! This is an absolutely ridiculous and horrific trope to perpetuate, not only in literature but in the field of psychology, where this archetypal model is still used. Nothing could be more untrue than the notion that women of this age are harmful, irrelevant, or without vivaciousness and vibrancy.

In fact, women in the satisfaction phase are the most precious and unique type of people we have on the planet. Considering that only two other mammalian species — killer whales and pilot whales — go through menopause and continue living long afterward, postmenopausal women are an exquisite evolutionary rarity.

In this stage of life, we occupy a space that no other human gets to experience: we are no longer on the hook for procreation, no longer expected to be responsible for raising children, and we are free to explore our personhood outside of the constant pressure of this paradigm. Men never reach this stage — their fertility may decrease, but it never ceases completely. And younger women spend the fullness of their adulthood after puberty negotiating the choices of procreation (or not). After menopause we are also no longer subject to the constant monthly hormonal fluctuations of a menstruating body and all the effects that has on the psyche. In this stage, we belong only to ourselves and are able to share the wisdom we have amassed with other women around us.

Of course, for those of us women who have chosen to go the route of parenthood and who have children who choose the same, we enter a sacred and unique phase of life: grandparenthood.

Let me talk about grandmothers for a second. Grandmothers are perhaps the most important people we have on the planet! We humans are a complicated bunch, developmentally speaking. All other animals are able to survive on their own after a relatively short period of growth. Humans are the only ones who take so much time to develop enough to fend for themselves. Even after we begin individuating from our parents, around the time of puberty, we still need a familial support group in order to get us to the finish line of adulthood and a fully formed prefrontal cortex.

Here is a quick Freudian aside. Basically, parents and children have sticky psychology. Whatever parents demonstrate to young children in the household ultimately determines the psychological makeup of their behavior and understanding of the world. In short, dear parents, it is impossible not to leave an indelible mark on the psyche of your children.

As adults, all the psychological and spiritual work we choose to undertake is inevitably for the purpose of undoing the damage of our youth. The parent/child dynamic is quite literally what keeps the field of psychology alive and therapists in business! While I understand the heartbreak of this truth, it is the privilege of all of us when we are grown to take whatever lessons we were saddled with as children and use them as grist for the mill of spiritual, emotional, and psychological growth. It's what gives us character, makes us who we are, and, ultimately, makes whatever experiences we had as children worth it.

Grandmothers are perfect in this regard. We do not have the same responsibilities as parents and are relatively free from this complicated psychological dynamic. We simply get to enter into the young person's life to sprinkle some fairy dust, unconditional love, and the magic of timeless wisdom. If we don't have grandchildren of our own, we often still have young women in our life who look to our wisdom for support, answers, and insights. Remember, when we were in the earlier phases of womanhood, we had a whole world to explore and important choices to make. Anything we can do to impart the wisdom of our lifetime to women younger than us is not just our privilege as the Satisfied Woman, but our responsibility.

We know that it is not easy to be a woman. Our choices are complicated and multifaceted, especially in this day and age, when more choices are available to us and the road map to feminine satisfaction has not yet become a well-worn path. We are the ones laying that pathway down and offering the women who come after us some illumination on what may otherwise be a very dark road. In the absence of well-known heroes and a litany of satisfied examples, we must become those things for other women.

I think about a dear friend of mine who forged a fabulously

successful career in science, one of the few women in the profession. She was a maverick in her field and rose to the ranks of prominence in museums and universities on both coasts. Of course, she was often the only woman in the room for her entire career and was typically in charge of all the employees who worked with her, who were usually men. As a woman who never married and chose not to have children, she has now entered the age of retirement and is using her time to give back to her community. Her fulfillment lies in being of service to other women who are awestruck by her powerful choices and singular accomplishments. She was my professor in my undergraduate studies, and after twenty-five years of friendship, she still inspires me today.

As I've learned by watching my friend, the gift of the satisfaction phase is keen discernment. We carry enough life history at this point to be unfailingly sure about what makes us the Satisfied Woman and what does not. And our age and wisdom at this stage mean that we're no longer ruled by other people's opinions, knowing that we have already lived through many of the larger consequences of life.

No matter what choices we make in our lifetime, as the Satisfied Woman beyond menopausal age we have amassed experiences that no other woman before us has. Women of even a few generations ago (our own grandmothers, for example) were never free to make the choices we were afforded as the incept, the sensate, and the initiate. We live in a brave, new, exciting world. And in this later chapter of our life, we get to be the beacons of light who show others the way of the Satisfied Woman.

The Only Constant Is Change

Women not only experience what I call the ISIS phases throughout our life — inception, sensation, initiation, satisfaction — which are governed by biology, hormonal changes, and time, but for several decades we also have a monthly cycle that affects our mood, outlook, and attitude. Until menopause, women are unfailingly reminded of our womanhood every twenty-eight days or so. We are confronted by the blood that symbolizes our ability to create life. And the hormonal changes that occur in that four-week period color the expression of our psyche. Depending on where we are in our cycle, we may find ourselves more or less emotional, more or less interested in sex, and more or less capable of putting up with nonsense. Our body cleans house during our period, and we may find ourselves doing the same thing, taking out the physical, mental, emotional, and spiritual trash we have collected over the past few weeks. There are moments of our cycle when it is easier to make decisions and moments when we have a hard time going with the flow.

There's no doubt: this is a woman thing.

Men don't have to navigate a constantly changing brain and biology. And — make no mistake — these monthly hormonal changes profoundly affect our psyche. Estrogen and serotonin are biologically linked. When our estrogen decreases at the end of our menstrual cycle, so does our serotonin, which increases the potential for anxiety and depression. The end of our menstrual cycle psychologically prompts more introspection, a greater need for closeness, and an intolerance for the intolerable. Moreover, during ovulation, we are both more desirous of sex and more sexually desirable! The beginning of our cycle often corresponds with more social behavior and an uplifted mood. Again, there are nuances to each of us as unique women.

In fact, women must get used to the one thing that is constant in our lives: change. Our desires may change from one moment to the next. So might our moods. We may be craving flannel and fleece one day and leather and lace the next. It has always been said that it's a woman's prerogative to change her mind; her own biology and psychology set her up for success amid change. This ease with constant change relies on a woman's connection to her intuitive emotions, which gives her the ability to seek out as much comfort as is possible within the flux. It's a never-ending process of internal and external recalibration that we are wise to lean into.

We can find incredible power in this constant cycle. There is no stasis for the woman. There is no status quo. We are never content to simply let things ride. Our bodies are in a perpetual state of preparedness for birth, growth, and death, and psychologically we need to be, too. We need to be ready to release what no longer serves us, take on that which does, and constantly reevaluate our surroundings for maximum comfort and ease. This is how paradigms shift, growth is achieved, and satisfaction reached.

The Feminine Clock

Women are governed by time. There is no putting off the monthly cycle. We can't keep the baby in our belly until we are ready. There is no procrastination when it comes to menopause. And the biologically predetermined cycles and phases of our life mean that we actually have limited time within which to undertake certain matters, so we have to be very calculated about when to start and end things.

This comes up in our bodies, our hearts and minds, our careers, our families, our relationships…everywhere. While the masculine is governed by the question "How?," the feminine is ruled by the question "When?" The masculine loves purpose-driven direction, but the feminine determines exactly how long that direction should take and when it needs to be complete.

It is much easier for the masculine to put things off. A funny joke circulating among my friends is this: "Ladies, if you've asked a man to do something, you don't have to keep reminding him every six months!" Except we do. We don't have time to waste. Urgency is part of our biology.

So when we ask for timelines, we actually need them to be both set and heeded. It is not pushy or demanding to ask for that.

We're not nagging when we follow up. You've heard of that biological clock? Well, it ticks for the feminine woman in all aspects of her life. She feels every moment of every day, and that certainty ticking away within her body needs to be honored by her outer world and relationships. Time agreements that are honored by those who make them give her confidence and security, so that she can *relax* and enjoy the time she does have, without additional worry and stress.

Consider the Hindu goddess Kali. Her name comes from the Sanskrit root *kāla*, which means "time." Kali is literally the keeper of time and has dominion over growth, destruction, and change. There is nothing more primordially feminine than this fierce goddess who is known for unceremoniously chopping off heads. She is unafraid to destroy, because she knows that growth is inherent in change and life is inherent in death. As the keeper of time, Kali's heart beats just as a woman's does: with anticipation. Kali's work never stops, and she halts her beheadings only at the sight of her star-crossed lover, Shiva. As the masculine principle of the universe, Shiva is equipped to rest, pause, stop, and lie in repose. That inertia is what finally brings Kali to a halt...at least for a brief moment before the inevitable progression of time and its decay continues.

Time doesn't stop for us women. Time doesn't slow down. Our whole body and psyche exist to obey time. And while we're on the clock, all we want is more. If the constant question of the woman is "When?," then the statement of femininity is "*More.*" Because we do want it all! As the generators of life, the wielders of the life force, and the creators of pleasure, we live in bodies that want every sensual experience they can handle. We are designed to delight in *feeling*...our emotions, the life energy flowing through our veins, life itself. What woman doesn't want more of that? We are hardwired for it — it is in our biology, in our psyche, in our souls.

But we don't have time to waste. Not only do we always want more, we want it *now*. Now is the only time that is given to us.

Tomorrow may hold a different hormonal balance. Next week may bring different intuitive emotions to the fore. Next year may catapult us into a different phase of life altogether. For the procrastinators in your life (or for your own procrastinating tendencies), be clear that there is no procrastination for the feminine. Give yourself permission to demand timeliness, question delays, and ask clarifying questions about the things that are important to you. Your time is valuable; your essential femininity relies on it. We are on the clock. And we are here to unleash our wild, creative feminine energy upon the world and live the most satisfied life possible.

5

Healing the Feminine Psyche

A woman's soul is a vast ocean of secrets, dreams, and hopes. This is where she harbors her deepest desires, unspoken wishes, and the pieces of herself that have been broken throughout her lifetime. The soul — the unconscious part of our psyche — is the reservoir of all we keep hidden from the world, even from ourselves. It is within our feminine soul that we keep locked away all that makes us powerful, graceful, embodied, and pleasure filled.

That lock is strong, reinforced through cultural expectations, our upbringing, familial norms, and societal structures. For us women, the secrets of our femininity may be so well guarded — like a personal Fort Knox — that we rarely peek inside or dare to dream that the contents could be set free. As little girls, perhaps we admired and saw ourselves in the beautiful princesses in Disney movies (which, thank goodness, feature more diversity in recent years). Within the colorful worlds of fantasy and fairy tale, we could give free rein to all the hopes, dreams, and expectations of our little girl hearts. Our imaginations were fed — nurtured — with the idea that we are creative, strong, cherished, worthy, powerful, joyful, and meant to be supported (no, saved!) by the handsome masculine on his brilliant white charger.

Or, in my case, a big black motorcycle.

There is no end to the irony of life, and even as we want to shy away from the clichéd connections between our childhoods and what we experience and expect as adults, it is impossible to escape the inevitability that lies buried within our unconscious. For me, my father was an adventurer, a thrill seeker, a living-life-large kind of guy. He called me his "little buddy," and he loved to share his joy with me by periodically picking me up from school on his motorcycle to journey through the Colorado mountains to a little place called Tiny Town, where for an afternoon my little girl imagination could live in little girl houses in a town that was built for me — safe, playful, and wonderful.

It is no wonder, then, that decades later the masculine counterpart who came to save the adult Alanna — and the little girl inside her — rides a big black motorcycle and loves thrill seeking and adventure just as much as I do.

As much as we may resist this truth: all little girls grow up to fall in love with their fathers.

Or at least what they perceive and experience their fathers to be.

This is even true of abrasive, abandoning, abusive fathers. No matter the father experience, the psyche is hardwired to search for and replicate it…even if, on a conscious level, we desperately don't want to! Our entire childhood provides the blueprint for our adult self, to the extent that we unconsciously seek out and repeat our childhood relationships, experiences, assumptions, and attitudes as grown-ups.

When we are children, we have undeveloped brains and a very limited understanding of the people and complex relationships around us. We only get part of the picture, and the earlier we look back into the history of our lives, the more basic and incomplete that picture is. Before we reach eighteen months, we have already made big decisions about the nature of our world: *Is it safe? Am I cared for?* The answers to those fundamental questions get locked into our tiny baby brains, and they determine our most fundamental assumptions about our world and the people around us. Those early experiences with our caregivers reinforce that either we are safe and loved or we are not. And we carry those assumptions throughout our adult lives.

A little further on in our childhood experience, we witness the nature of intimate partnership (or lack thereof) between our parents or caregivers. We see the masculine and feminine in action... or the dysfunction therein. We witness examples of emotional regulation or dysregulation, conflict and repair or disrepair, cherishing and respect or breakdown and contempt. We take those early lessons in all the ways that our caregivers demonstrate life, love, and family, and we bury them deep in the lockbox of our souls, and we label them "truths."

But here's the thing about those truths. They are personal truths, not universal truths. And they are true only *because we continue to reinforce them and live them throughout our lives.* This is why we end up in the same type of relationship and circumstance over and over again, playing out the same dysfunctions, just with different people. As we continually reinforce our perceptions about what we believe, the *real* truth about our world remains even more tightly and securely locked within us. The real truth being that our perceptions are rooted in our own psychology, and we have the power to heal and reveal something even more holistic, more complete — more true — than we ever thought possible.

While it may be difficult to digest the fact that our adult interactions, relationships, and circumstances are based on a five- or seven-year-old (or earlier!) mindset, it is the truth. This reflects a basic understanding of psychology and prompts the work of therapy, healing, and repair that we embark on as adults. Our journey toward being fully embodied feminine adult women begins when we are little girls. And as we live into our adult years, we reenact childhood mistakes, misunderstandings, and missed opportunities from our youth, giving ourselves the platform for potential transformation, evolution, and understanding.

The full empowerment of our femininity is only possible with the reconciliation of these childhood assumptions, wounds, and traumas. We all have them — especially as women of this modern world. While the magnitude of our personal experiences varies, whatever the trauma, it affects every individual in profound ways. It is important here to remember that the details of the trauma are not necessarily what's most significant, but what it meant to us and how it became stored within us. What is most useful to understand is that no one gets through childhood unscathed — least of all little girls.

As we've said, all children occupy the feminine polarity for the first ten years or so of life. Polarities differentiate with the flood of hormones around puberty, and children who grow into feminine women have early experiences of life that are unique to girls and similar challenges to face as adults. The masculine patriarchal world inherently places less value on the young female. Think of entire cultures where the male child is strongly preferred. Or of harmful stereotypes that perpetuate the patriarchal narratives that girls are weak, meek, and overly emotional and that "boys will be boys" (excusing bad behavior) and "boys don't cry" (reinforcing emotional suppression in young male children). Even beloved Disney princesses of yore reinforced disadvantageous narratives of helplessness, dependence, and lack of agency.

But the answer does not lie in offering masculine narratives and opportunities to young girls. Rather, we must demonstrate, empower, and center the incredible strengths of character embodied by the healthy feminine. Remember, it is not *what* the feminine does, but *how*. Give us a Disney princess who is a loudmouthed mechanic who uses her creative wiles to win the funny car race and talk her opponents into a collaborative effort to win back her best friend. Show me the unkempt wild woman at home in the forest, cooking her own wild-caught meal, when the wide-eyed prince stumbles along and cannot help but feel joy and pleasure in this strong woman's presence. Tell me the tale of the magical young girl whose intuitive and emotional gifts are misunderstood at first, but ultimately are valued by the community so highly that she is honored as the queen of the land.

Gender differences are OK. Gender differentials are not.

And no matter what sex a child is assigned at birth or what psychic polarity they ultimately embody, it is worthwhile for all young children to understand the inherent dynamics, value, valuable differences, and common elements of both polarities. Remember, every human has *both* polarities within them, and it is not healthy for any of us to devalue any part of ourself, try to repress any element of who we are, or deny very real and valid elements of our psyche. Everyone deserves the right to be free and authentically themselves, in whatever unique expression feels most genuine to them.

It's when we value the qualities of the masculine *over* the feminine that children learn to repress, judge, and shame. This hierarchical devaluing is what ultimately causes and reinforces inequality for women of all ages, and it complicates the presence of femininity within men, too. As healthy humans, our ability to navigate either polarity at particular times is essential. When feminine qualities are repressed, judged, or shamed in any of us, *we all suffer.* It is OK for the little boy to cry. It is wonderful for the little girl to play with trucks. And as our young children navigate a healthy representation of both the masculine and the feminine around them, as they witness healthy dynamics between the two, as they learn that both are inherently valuable, then no matter which polarity they ultimately lean more fully into, they will have access to both and will respect and cherish each one, too.

While such a scenario is ideal — and I hope we make headway toward that becoming the reality for our children as we move forward — for most of you reading this book, that was not the case growing up. Too many of us grew up with the shame of being feminine girls. We were relegated to playing with dolls featuring unrealistic body shapes (although thank you, Greta Gerwig, for forever changing the Barbie narrative!) and aspiring to be hopeless princesses without our own agency or domain. It's time to heal the feminine psyche, and to do that we must enter our psychological time machines and rewrite the narrative from back to front, so that we become the most healthful, skillfully embodied, and empowered feminine possible.

The work of healing the unconscious — really, of healing our childhood wounds — is not just the work of the feminine woman but the privilege of anyone in their lifetime. Of course, for us as women, this healing of the inner girl child is precious, essential, and a pathway to tremendous transformation and self-acceptance, self-governance, self-understanding, and self-empowerment. When we are able to stand in our power as feminine women, we offer our strength to others not only to be powerful but also to confidently embark on their own healing journeys. Changing the world around us is actually an inside job. So as we look more deeply at the common wounds of the feminine psyche and how we might navigate our inner landscape to recover our greatest gifts, know that this is not just about you as an individual satisfied sister. When we heal ourselves, we give permission to the feminine around us to heal, too. May our own inner work bring safety and satisfaction to the other women we encounter. It is in this spirit that we draw energy for the journey.

The Core Wound of the Feminine

We are all wounded. While that may sound fatalistic, cynical, or like a total bummer, it is simply part of the human psychological condition. And it is one of the great privileges of our lifetime to discover our wounds in order to understand, heal, and resolve them. This psychological work, also sometimes known as *shadow work*, allows us to mine the depths of our darkness and bring what we find there into the light. Often, what we find surprises us. The more we look into the darkness, the more we realize that we bump into certain of the same roadblocks again and again and again.

There is often one thing that consistently trips us up on our journey toward the light, one thing that dominates our unconscious and colors everything we see and experience. More than likely, the thing that stops us over and over was embedded deep inside of us so long ago, we may not even have a rational or complete memory of what happened. But a part of us does. Everything we experience in this lifetime is stored in our psyche, to be retrieved when we least expect it, usually when it has the greatest potential to reveal some inner truth.

That truth being that we are complex human beings who deserve to be loved and accepted and who ultimately thrive in healthy relationship — to ourself and to others. At some point in our early childhood, even before two years of age, we come to stunning conclusions about ourself and our world. From interactions with our primary caregivers, we determine whether the world is friendly or not, supportive or not, safe or not. We learn whether we can depend on others, whether they help us get our basic and most urgent needs met, and whether they are to be trusted. All the information we acquire in this infantile state — long before our brain is fully developed — gets locked into our psyche and filed as "the truth." What we determine about our own safety, self-worth, and surroundings then becomes true for us — throughout our life.

It seems incredible and unfair that experiences so early on leave such an indelible mark on our souls. Our first experiences in relationship with our caregivers ultimately shape our life, coloring our behavior, expectations, and the outcomes of every relationship thereafter. These early experiences help us to form our ability to emotionally regulate ourselves and seek comfort when necessary from those we trust. If there is no comfort or no trust, then emotional regulation becomes difficult, and we either shut down or fall apart under stress. Psychologists file this phenomenon under the category of "attachment"; it is the foundation for how we experience and deal with our own emotions and how we relate to others throughout life. If our primary caregivers offered us consistent positive connection, gave us the safety and security to explore ourselves and our world, taught us healthy boundaries of behavior, and provided a calm and loving environment, then we had a greater opportunity to develop healthy, secure attachments to others as children and later as adults.

If our caregivers failed to provide adequate comfort, modeled unclear or unhealthy boundaries, demonstrated a lack of connection, and provided a chaotic and variable emotional environment, then we are more likely to develop along the spectrum of insecure, avoidant, or anxious attachments to others. This is where we see difficulty with emotional regulation, challenges in trusting others and being vulnerable, and similar behaviors that make relating to other people and getting our emotional needs met a challenge. Of course, each of us falls somewhere on the spectrum of attachment on the basis of our life experiences and circumstances, and the way we relate and attach to others may change and evolve over time, especially as we embark on our personal shadow work.

Interestingly — or perhaps not, given all we know about femininity as it has evolved through patriarchal culture — research shows gender differences in how children react when they do not have a secure attachment style. Typically, boys lash out and exhibit more aggressive, disruptive, and attention-seeking behavior, while girls tend to show more dependent, compliant, and fawning (apologetic, making everything OK) behavior. While it's difficult to know whether it is nature or nurture that fosters these differences in young children, the important point is that *there are differences*. As adults, we tend to see more avoidant attachment behavior from men and more anxious attachment behavior from women. This follows the biological imperative for women, who anxiously seek long-term, committed partners and caregivers for their children.

Perhaps you are familiar with the idea in the dating world that women are perpetually ready to commit. After all, Beyoncé does strongly suggest that "if you like it then you should have put a ring on it." This ingrained feminine need for commitment has psychological and biological roots, and the instincts that drive it are powerful and pervasive. Commitment ensures survival. It ensures safety, security, and protection of our place in our world. It gives us reassurance that the children we carry — and whom we are ultimately responsible for long term — are also provided for. And whether or not we have children, the need for commitment is encoded at a cellular level and encased within our feminine psyche.

Luckily, in healthy and securely attached bonding, both men and women exhibit and value the need for commitment, connection, and healthy attachment to each other. In a balanced and optimized state, both genders understand that more is gained from partnership, cooperation, and collaboration than from isolation. Among the myriad benefits of a successful relationship, the most important may be the coregulation of our nervous system, which occurs when the interaction between people results in a beneficial biological and behavioral effect on the nervous system, essentially resetting it and reducing stress. This has wide-reaching effects on our psychology (improved mental health), emotions (better regulation and resilience), and physiology (reduced stress and inflammation, improved cardiovascular health, and increased longevity).

The early impressions of our world and how we determined as infants the best way to get our most basic needs met form a perpetual shadow over our lives. And while we may not remember the circumstances or may have a hard time creating a clear, accurate picture of our early life, its effects are felt in nearly every important interaction we have. Essentially, as babies, we learn very quickly which types of basic behavior elicit the responses we need. Our survival literally depends on it. If we discover that being sweet and apologetic gets us more food or if lashing out and throwing a tantrum brings us the attention we seek, then we grow into similar patterns of behavior as adults in every relationship — and particularly in intimate partnership.

And thank goodness we knew early on the appropriate behavioral strategies to help us cope! What an incredible survival mechanism! We can thank our early selves for adapting and getting our needs met in the best way possible under the circumstances. However, there comes a time that we may want to revise those strategies to achieve healthier patterns of behavior and relationship as adults.

For the feminine woman, as I mentioned earlier, the patterns of behavior we adopt tend toward apology, anxiety, neediness, meekness, and subservience. We caretake others' emotional needs before our own, trying to placate sufficiently to get the love we seek. We need that love. We need that belonging. We crave that connection. Our lives literally depend on it. We are not safe without it. Especially as infants, we must be taken care of, provided for, and cherished. If we were properly taken care of and given all the love, support, and secure attachment possible, then we thrive as young feminine children and have the best shot at growing into confidently feminine women.

But even if we missed out on love, care, and cherishing as infants, there is always hope. By delving into the depths of our unconscious, we discover the roots of this core wound. And once we find those roots, the brain and the psyche are wondrous in their ability to adapt and heal. The neural pathways of the brain can reroute their previous assumptions about the world and reveal a revised reality: that it can be a safe, secure, and loving place. Through our intentional, positive relationships with others, we are given the opportunity to create new truths for ourselves, including the fact that we have inherent worthiness and that we can be safe, secure, and cherished in the world we create as confident, adult feminine women.

The Mother Wound: Enmeshment and Abandonment

Our earliest relationship is with our mother. Growing inside her womb gives us the first sense of connection to another human being. Since we are all hardwired for connection, this innate closeness to our mother nourishes our growing soul.

What happens after birth, however, is a different story.

Inherent in the birth process is a disconnection, a separation from the one human who up to that point was entirely responsible for our growth, health, safety, and security. Once we leave the womb, we navigate a life of meaningful connections, missed connections, or failed connections. As we've discussed, we use our infantile means to get our needs met in the best way possible, and the initial responsibility to meet those needs usually falls to mother. Traditionally, she is the one who continues to feed us, as her body and biology have evolved to do so.

Of course, individual stories develop from there. There is no one way to mother.

Our mother may have risen to the occasion and provided all the connection, love, and nurturing necessary to foster our healthy growth and attachment. Or our mother may have been incapable of doing so, for whatever reason. She may have had other traumas or challenges in her own life that thwarted her ability to tend to our early needs. Whether she was present or not, loving or not, nurturing or not, whatever our mother demonstrated for us in our early childhood years has lasting effects on our feminine psyche, and we bring those unmet needs into our relationships as adults. All too often, parents are not properly attuned to their children's needs and fail to provide for or respond to the demands of the child in a way that is satisfying to the child.

No matter the circumstances, the presence of *mother* lives large in the human psyche. It is one of the primary archetypes that is present for all humans. Mother is a universal truth. And the recognition of and reconciliation with mother is something we all must contend with. Our impressions of and assumptions about mother are pervasive in our psychology throughout our life. For the feminine woman, it tends to show up as one of two primary complexes: enmeshment or abandonment.

For the mother who has difficulty separating her own needs and identity from those of her children, there is a likelihood of *enmeshment.* We see this when the mother obsesses over the child, making her own life about that of her daughter — identifying with the daughter's challenges, achievements, activities, and attitudes. When the daughter cannot individuate beyond the mother's identity, or when the mother sabotages the daughter's attempts at independence, then it becomes difficult to tease out one psyche from the other. This may appear as a mother and daughter being "best friends," or as the mother being overly involved in the daughter's life, or as the borderline or narcissistic mother being unable to tolerate any independence or individual personality traits from the daughter. In this more detrimental scenario, emotions are fused, boundaries are lacking, and the child's sense of okayness is dependent on the approval of the mother. No matter the many ways enmeshment appears, its effects on the young woman show up as an inability to see herself separately from the mother and to fully develop into her own feminine womanhood. As an adult, the daughter's enmeshment arises as a continued inappropriate identity with the mother — constantly checking in for approval, trying to live up to the mother's standards or ideals — or as continued unclear boundaries and emotional dependence in relationship to others.

On the opposite end of the spectrum is *abandonment* by the mother. This isn't apparent only in the extreme case of the mother not being present in the child's life, but also manifests in any way the child experiences her needs not being met and a lack of emotional connection with or responsiveness by the mother. This tends to produce anxiety and neediness in the daughter as she seeks the comfort and closeness she knows keep her safe, both emotionally and physically. As the daughter grows into an adult woman, she brings this anxiety and neediness into her relationships with her intimate partners and also, potentially, with her own children. Or there may be the opposite effect, where the abandoned daughter becomes the abandoner, withdrawing her love and care from those around her.

Whatever the circumstances of the mother/daughter relationship, if needs were not properly met, martyrdom tends to develop in the psyche. We see this in feminine women who often displace their own needs to take care of the needs of those around them. Whether it stems from neediness and anxiety or from blurred emotional boundaries and dependence, the result is largely the same, and we tend to fall into the trap as adult women of subjugating our needs to satisfy those of others. Particularly when our needs are not met as young girls, we overcompensate by overdoing the nurturing and caring we felt we missed as children.

We have this ingrained idea that a mother "should" be nurturing to her children, that she "should" be caring, present, loving, and supportive. And while those are, indeed, qualities of parenthood (in a parent of either gender), those qualities may not be present in the specific person who becomes our mother. Although all women are capable of becoming mothers (whether by pregnancy, marriage, or adoption), not all women have the skills or temperament of motherhood. Just because a woman enters into that phase of life does not automatically imbue her with the skills needed for parenthood. And though we *expect* mothers to behave with these qualities, we cannot ask of people what they are not capable of giving or what is not in their character. We do not ask a mechanic to bake us cookies — that is not their skill set! The mechanic may simply never be (or want to be) a baker. A woman may simply never have the skills and qualities of a mother.

Of course, this is not a pill that a young child swallows easily or even understands. It is only as adult women that we may look back — with our fully formed prefrontal cortex, our ability to self-regulate our emotions and triggers, and the strength and agency to stand in our power — and be able to understand *who our mother really was as a woman*. She was placed under the same challenging constraints of masculine ideals and patriarchal oppression that we ourselves face. She likely had a childhood that mirrored the same things she later mirrored for us. And since no young girl gets through childhood unscathed, that is likely true for our mother, too. Even if we wished things had been different, they weren't. There is no point in arguing our reality or trying to negotiate with the past. Our work now is to heal our feminine psyche as adult women moving forward. In this way, we hope to recalibrate our internal patterns, habits, and traumas — and in the process to give our daughters or the young women in our lives a new lens with which to view the mother.

In order to heal our mother wound, we must surrender any thought we have that things "should" have been different. We've got to stop "should-ing" ourselves! Whoever our mother was to us as a young child has brought us to who we are today. The lessons, even if they might have been painful, can give us the capacity to discern and understand from a compassionate perspective.

We want something different. Now. And moving forward.

The key to having this is what we likely missed as a young woman coming of age: a ritual that initiated us into fully capable adulthood. The two most important elements of these lost coming-of-age rituals are that the youngster is now viewed as a full-fledged woman by her community and by her own reckoning and that the mother is given back to herself. The young woman is now responsible for mothering herself. This places the agency firmly within the young feminine psyche, retrieving any lost or discordant tendrils of attachment from the mother's psyche. No longer does the young woman depend on the mother for emotional validation. She seeks her own emotional approval internally. In effect, she reaches back into her psyche, finds the small girl within, and nurtures her by giving her whatever she needed and missed. She is self-responsible, self-aware, and self-confident. She approves of and loves herself, perhaps better than her biological mother did!

And as the biological mother is released from the duties of motherhood, she is allowed to return to her natural polarity, no longer on the hook for providing for and nurturing the young child. This isn't to say that the family unit is lost or that suddenly the young lady is cast out on her own. It's a psychological shift, not a locational shift. Now the dynamic between the two women can be completely in the feminine. Now the learning can be on the level of how to be a woman with agency, instead of how to grow up as a child in the world. Rather than the continually reinforced structure and protection of parents, the young woman now needs demonstrations of the healthy masculine and feminine from her caregivers and community so that she may enter the inception phase and begin to explore for herself the kind of woman she can be — fully satisfied, self-aware, and in accord with her own evolving feminine psyche.

The Father Wound: Dealing with Daddy Issues

I can feel the resistance in many readers even as I'm about to write these words: women inevitably fall in love with a replica of their fathers. There. I said it. As cliché as it may sound, as much as we may deny this truth, and as much effort as we put into trying to make this prophecy *not* come true, psychologically speaking, it is almost fated. Whether our fathers were present in our lives or not, whether we participate in heteronormative relationships or not, when we look across the span of intimate relationships as adult women, what we find is a common thread that relates back to our early childhood experiences with the masculine parent or caregiver.

I know we live in the twenty-first century and tired tropes of the nuclear family are being more and more challenged and revised. No matter the familial conditions of our upbringing, the presence (or not) of our father leaves a lasting, indelible mark on the psyche. Though the polarity dynamic of parents generally shifts toward the masculine while children under ten occupy the feminine, there are times the young child sees interactions between caregivers and other adults that suggest oppositional polarity and demonstrate the relationship between masculine and feminine. Not to mention the stories, fairy tales, myths, and legends of youth that offer ideas and insights into how adult relationships work. And at some point, as the child grows up and the parents shift back into opposing dynamics, they have an even greater opportunity to witness adults' modeled behavior and glean insights into the treatment of one polarity by another.

In single-parent or single-caregiver households, the absence of the opposite polarity is felt, and chances to witness how the two polarities interact may be limited and perhaps give an "absent" feeling to the missing dynamic. In households with two parents of the same gender, opposing relational polarities between two humans still thrive as the child grows up and the couple is able to move back into their primary polarities (remember, every human has both polarities, and typically intimate relationships feature people of differing primary polarities). Because of the intrinsic nature of duality within every human psyche, children in any type of household structure have opportunities to witness and draw conclusions about the relational nature and value of the two polarities. If we focus on the interactions with and impressions of the masculine on a young girl, we discover profound things about her nascent psyche. Remember, her perception is limited, because early psychological and brain development allows her to understand just so much, and much of it is relegated to what is most important to the youngster: *Am I safe? Am I cared for? Am I accepted? Am I loved?*

One of the earliest relationships young girls develop is with their fathers or with their most masculine caregivers. The young girl wants nothing more than to be at the center of her father's world. She longs to be the apple of his eye, the object of his affection, and she hopes that he gets wrapped around her little finger. Few things are more nourishing to the young girl's psyche than the unconditional love, affection, and attention of a caring father in his healthy masculine. He shows her what it means to have the love of a big masculine heart and the protection and providership of a strong masculine man. Or at least that is the ideal in the young feminine psyche.

Unfortunately, many of us had fathers who, in one way or another, were not in alignment with our needs. For whatever reason, it may have been beyond their capacity to provide the nurturing, structure, and care necessary for us as children. We must also take into account the difficulty of their own upbringing in a distorted masculine culture, where they may have been taught the doctrine of denial of emotions and connection to others. Men are sometimes given the narrative that they have to be emotionless providers who miss opportunities for heartfelt connection and presence as fathers. Whatever the condition or assumptions the father is imbued with, the way in which he relates to his daughter creates the template for how she relates to her masculine counterparts as an adult.

Yes, we are here to talk about daddy issues.

The proverbial daddy issues are merely the way we learned to relate to the masculine as young girls, which created assumptions about our relationship to the masculine that then got locked in as "the truth" within our feminine psyche. We cling to Dad's leg as he leaves for the long work trip, begging him to stay…only to then feel resentful when our adult masculine counterpart leaves for his own work trip. We are told as young girls that we need to "smile and be cute" for daddy…and then, as adults, we assume that men only want us to smile and be pretty. As frustrating and inconvenient as it may be, it is also remarkable how directly our childhood experiences with our father are reflected in our adult relationships.

Here is the bad news and the good news: we are wounded through relationship, and we are also healed through relationship.

Just like our mother, our father likely did his best with the psychological baggage he was carrying at the time. No matter how our father treated us, we learned and made assumptions about what it took to receive his love, to feel safe in his presence, to warrant his cherishing and protection. We adapted in very smart ways, perhaps endearing ourselves to him, behaving in a desirable manner to garner favor, or doing what was necessary based on a complex recipe of interactions that revealed the best way to gain his love. If our father was emotionally reticent, our behavior may have played out as needy, anxious, or demanding in order to incite *any* emotion from him, just to feel some sense of connection. If our dad was rarely or never present, then his absence loomed as large in our psyches as the absence of the knighted savior we longingly waited for in our favorite fairy tales. If our father or primary masculine caregiver was harmful, was abusive, or created an unsafe environment, then safety would be at the heart of our needs in relationships moving forward.

Every young girl longs to be saved. And safe.

Safe from the oppression and expectations placed on her by those around her. Safe from the constrictions of what it means to be a girl in this culture. Safe from the straitjacket of meek and mild emotions deemed acceptable by the world. Safe from the assumptions of smallness, the expectations of weakness, and the demands to be everything to everyone. Safe from any kind of sexual abuse, subjugation, or objectification. The young feminine psyche imagines that her father — the most masculine presence in her life — is capable of protecting her from these herculean challenges. Because if he can't do it, then who can? And if he doesn't, well, then, our inner feminine fades into the background, to be protected by our own hardened masculine mask.

It's a complicated setup. Fathers are only human, parenthood is tough, the patriarchy is tougher, and little girls are competing with a perpetual narrative of submission and oppression while simultaneously exploring what it means to be feminine. First, as young children naturally in the feminine polarity, their needs are entirely dependent on caregivers. They *must* be provided for and protected. As the young girl comes of age, she may need less safety and security in the literal sense, but she still craves protection and her father's love. When she doesn't receive this, where is it to be made up? How does she create it so that she can generate the Four Keys in her life?

Healing the feminine psyche requires in part that we establish safety, security, and the ability to trust and be cherished. We must trust our ability to relate to others, including our ability to choose people worthy of relating to. Oftentimes, in our trauma and confusion around the needs unmet by the father, we find ourselves second-guessing our intuitive skills in reading others, particularly the masculine. We overlook bad behavior; we excuse unkindness and justify it by deprecating ourselves. The anxiety of the feminine psyche that searches for the lost love of the father sometimes seeks it in situations where it is ultimately unavailable.

We live this every time a boss walks all over our personal needs or when we place the needs of our family above our own. We play this out in intimate relationships when we apologize for an infraction committed by the other person. It is a common behavior, easy to trace back to the unmet needs of the little girl within us. Amazingly, that little girl has fierce wisdom. She determined early on what behaviors were necessary to keep her safe.

We are not little girls anymore.

As adult women, it is our privilege to take back our agency, empower our emotions, ensure our own needs are met, and never second-guess our intuition again. Essentially, when we project the role of our father onto another person, we need to de-role our original masculine caregiver, give him back to himself, extract his looming presence from our psyche, and find the capability within to protect, cherish, and lead *ourselves* to satisfaction. When we re-father ourselves, we stop outsourcing our agency to others who are unworthy of the responsibility. We reclaim our intuitive skills and our capacity to cherish our emotional experiences. And we develop the discernment necessary to keep people in our lives who enhance our feminine essence while boldly kicking out anyone who does not.

Consider this process a fortification of the feminine essence, like building a protective fence around a house to keep the harmful characters at bay, but kindly allowing into this space the ones who cherish us, those whom we trust, and those who make us feel safe and secure. We welcome those who have the capacity to mirror healthy relationships filled with love, compassion, acceptance, belonging, and connection. And we invite the mirrors of the healthy masculine to reflect back and appreciate our most powerful feminine essence.

The Wounding of Coming of Age

Along with the challenges of childhood and the unique struggles that a young girl's psyche confronts, we must also contend with the experience of coming of age. With the onset of puberty and menarche, the young lady suddenly contends with the transition from childhood to womanhood, and she needs to understand her changed status in the world and her new ability to create and bear life.

These are heavy truths for a young mind.

Few of us are properly prepared for it. Research reveals that the majority of women recognized the swift maturity required at the sign of their first period, but also reported negative associations with this event. And it is an event. For every young woman, it is a moment, an instant, prior to which she was a carefree child, and after the first sight of blood, she is suddenly a full-fledged woman capable of motherhood and all the responsibilities that entails. Culturally, we are ill-equipped for this transition, with the scant education young girls typically receive about their own bodies, not to mention the shy attempts of parents to demystify it. Pair that with the societal sanitizing of "female problems" and the shame associated with all things menstrual — bleeding through clothing, for example, and having to carry feminine products — and women tend to remember their coming-of-age experience in a difficult light.

It's a scary time for a young lady. Between the biological, social, and psychological connotations, becoming a woman is also fraught with overtones of sexuality. In an instant, the little girl becomes an object of potential desire. And the message is that not only is this entirely her responsibility, but also anything that happens to her body is her fault.

In the first season of the Paramount Network series *Yellowstone*, we see a flashback of Beth Dutton's mother filling her in on the harsh reality of life as a woman now that she's gotten her period. Her mother explains that because she loves her, it is time to toughen her up, to "turn her into the man that most men will never be." The mother tells her only daughter that suddenly, after this day, everything will be different.

How right she is.

While young men enjoy a slow slide into adulthood, sometimes never even crossing that amorphous psychological border, young women are forced over that boundary between the land of playful childhood and the realms of responsible adulthood, whether they like it or not. Not all young women take this border crossing well. Some rebel. Some revolt. But no matter the reaction, the event is impossible to ignore; it leaves an indelible impression on the feminine psyche. Every woman remembers the circumstances of her first period. Most associate it with how it was honored and celebrated...or not. And whether her mother was present...or not.

Most young girls have a desire for their mother to demystify menses, demonstrate femininity in its fullness, and show them the agency inherent in being a woman. Rightly or wrongly, girls generally have the impression that it is their mother who is meant to be there for them at this turning point, to revel in this momentous coming of age, to commemorate their entry into the next phase of life. But as long as menses remains a cultural mystery, femininity is repressed, and agency is lost by women in many circumstances, what is the mother to do? Society still perpetuates a cycle of trauma around womanhood — so we shame its onset. We leave the newly minted young girl confused about her worth with her changed status in society.

In many historical and current religious cultures and spiritual traditions, young women undergo a coming-of-age ceremony that denotes their new status as women. They are invited to leave behind the child they once were and step into their fullness as adults in their society. Sometimes, they are even further honored by being allowed to join other menstruating women for a time of reflection and communion during their bleed. Menstruation isn't always a shameful fact of the female. It used to be a prized status showing that these are the women who create and bear life, helping to preserve and elevate the community. And the young woman was then invited into this sacred society, to be a part of the community of women, to commune with them over all that is difficult and beautiful about being a woman.

Imagine how different your own coming-of-age experience would have been if this kind of ceremony had been given to you.

Instead, we are often cowed into adulthood, timidly hiding feminine products in our backpacks and tentatively trying on provocative clothing to *look* like a woman, even if we don't feel like one yet. We contend with the sexual advances of the opposite sex and the ridicule of our peers. Our bodies are often shamed, as much by ourselves as by others. And yet somehow, amid all this confusion, we are supposed to smile, be nice, and flourish as young women. This is a tall order. Certainly, one can understand the nature of teenage rebellion within these difficult and tumultuous circumstances. Of course, sometimes we opt for the opposite coping mechanism of trying to remain childlike, complacent, innocent in the eyes of our peers and family. There may be a sense of safety in the status of childhood that is far greater than the reality of womanhood.

No matter the reaction of the young woman to the onset of her period, a fairly clear demarcation exists. Forever there is the time before her period and the time after. She feels different, she is treated differently, and she is thrust into a world of new expectations that she may not welcome or be ready for. If the transition doesn't go smoothly, then it is grounds for shame and resentment. Shame around her status as a woman and resentment for the absence of ease in being a woman. It is a complicated matter, because what the young woman needs most at this time is a distinct demonstration of the fullness of the feminine and the power of womanhood. She needs role models. She needs guidance on how to walk the streets with her head held high, proud of who she is and without fear.

Her mother may not be able to give her this. Her community may not be able to, either.

But you, satisfied sister, you can be there for her. (And to the young women reading this book, it is our pledge that we will be there to celebrate and support you from here on out, to the best of our ability.)

While we continue to work toward greater societal change, the most important way we can heal our own coming-of-age wound is to be present for the daughters and other young women who look to us for inspiration. For those women who entered motherhood, it is likely you are around the initiation phase of your life by the time your daughter comes of age. This is an exceptional opportunity (thank you for that timing, nature) for you to step into your feminine capacity as a beacon for your young daughter, who is now in the inception phase. Encourage her to explore all that she wants to become by inviting her into the feminine fold. And for those of us who did not give birth to a daughter, we may still be demonstrative in this capacity to our stepdaughters, young women in our family, and others in our community.

Trust me when I say the young women are watching.

In the absence of a clear road map, young women look for any signs they can find of how to flourish as they explore their own femininity. Let us show them what it means to be an empowered, embodied, and enthused feminine woman. In this way, we heal ourselves, help each other, and lead those coming up behind us toward greater satisfaction as women.

Healing through Relationship

As humans, we are hardwired for relationship and connection. It is built into our DNA, our evolutionary biology, our brain structure, and our psyche. Nearly every aspect of our life centers around the success or failure of our relationships, and at times in human history, our very existence has been dependent on our human connections. This is not an overdramatization! Your DNA holds a record of your family history and relationships. Our brains contain mirror neurons that fire in response to the emotions and reactions of those around us — the biological basis of empathy, which kept us safe and alive throughout history and still protects and connects us today. Our psyche is ingrained with the primary relationship of the two polarities of masculine and feminine, not to mention the archetypal structures of family and social relationships. Our mental health and well-being are dependent on the quality of our external relationships.

Our human existence is based on relationship. This may be a difficult truth to digest in a day, age, and dominant culture that value independence, DIY attitudes, and self-reliance. We are taught to believe that we can do everything ourselves, including heal our emotional and psychological wounds from within. The idea that another might be necessary to the process of really healing and becoming whole feels rankling to any of us raised with this independent mindset. And for those of us who have studied certain styles of philosophy or Eastern mysticism, it might agitate us even further, as those methods place high value on the solitary journey. Pair any one of those ideas with the pride we derive from being single and self-reliant, and the concept of relationship generates even more resistance. But the fact is that for even the most self-sufficient among us, relationships are a fundamental function of life.

Case in point. I spent more than twenty years in Eastern spiritual pursuits, following the wisdom that it was through aloneness that I might become free of my haunting past and any demons therein. I meditated with the best of them, slept on beds of crystals, and even changed my last name to the Sanskrit word for "the power of aloneness": Kaivalya. After the first decade of study, the only thing I came to realize was that while I was able to gloss over the thoughts that permeated my psyche, I wasn't able to resolve them. I was still just as broken as when I started my spiritual and philosophical studies — I was just better at hiding my wounds and justifying them.

Through the study of depth psychology and learning about the relational nature of humanity and the psyche, I came to a different realization: there is only so much we can accomplish alone.

If we truly want personal freedom, if we truly want to love ourselves and be loved in return, if we truly seek purpose, passion, and meaning in this life, we cannot do it solo.

It may have actually been the last moments of the 2007 film *Into the Wild*, inspired by the book of the same name by Jon Krakauer, that shocked me into recognizing this truth. When the main character, who has been on a lengthy solitary journey into the wilderness, realizes he has eaten a poisonous plant and life is slowly fading from him, he pens one final piece of wisdom in his journal: "HAPPINESS ONLY REAL WHEN SHARED."

Though there is certainly much we can realize, resolve, and transform on our own, ultimately it is through intimate relationship that we derive the greatest depth of meaning. No matter how strong, friendships don't rise to the level of psychological investment necessary to create the change we seek. The reason why?

No one triggers us as deeply as our intimate partners.

Sure, friends may anger us, but those infractions are more easily resolved and released. Even our family members provide triggers for us regularly (think of holiday dinner gatherings), but the challenge there is that they were often present at the inception of our greatest wounds and remain locked in the patterning of our childhood themselves. Meanwhile, those we have intimately invested in — even for a short while — tend to bring up our most intense emotional responses from the very depths of our soul, in both positive and negative ways. It is in the retrieval of these deep emotions that we can find our greatest potential healing. They were initially stored there in early childhood and have been lying in wait until we became adults.

In short, we reenact the childhood scenarios encoded in our neural pathways through interactions with our adult intimate partnerships. When we make behavioral decisions in early childhood based on scenarios playing out with our caregivers, those behaviors effectively become the default setting moving forward. They get locked into our unconscious, only to be replayed when an adult interaction has the same vibe, the same feeling tone. At this point we meet the spring-loaded nature of the unconscious when emotional reactions arise unexpectedly, like a jack-in-the-box. Inevitably, the unconscious reveals itself in the most inconvenient moments. It brings forth triggered reactions, which are most easily identified when the level of emotion does not track with the seriousness of the event.

For example, you might be unconsciously triggered if you leave a heated argument suddenly and without warning, even though your partner is midsentence. It may be that as a child you witnessed an argument between your primary caregivers. They may have only been debating the price of milk, but the tension in the room was palpable enough to be scary and confusing to your young mind. The safest decision was to remove yourself from conflict and hide under the bed. For a three-year-old, that is an excellent decision to preserve your well-being! But for an adult, it is not. An adult who is emotionally regulated tolerates heated discussions — even arguments — with presence and consideration. In fact, it is often through conflict that we come to wonderful compromises with another as we search together for the best way to get everyone's needs met!

If, as adults, we hit an emotional trigger and experience a fight-or-flight response, then a really critical shift takes place in our brains. Rather than staying in the emotionally regulated (feeling everything fully while remaining calm and present), rational, decision-making part of the brain, aka the prefrontal cortex, the trigger moves us into the limbic system, where unconscious and uncontrolled emotions take over and our decisions become reactive. Physiologically, our heart rate increases, our breath quickens, and we may feel beads of sweat on our forehead — just as if we were being chased by a dangerous animal in the wild. The brain has not evolved to understand the differences between historical and modern threats. Physiologically, it reacts to the threat of a mountain lion with the same response as to the threat of losing a paycheck, being ridiculed in social settings, or having a conflict with a loved one. There is no differentiation! As amazing as the brain is, it does not know the difference between a real and a perceived experience. So when a traumatic event occurred in early childhood and the brain stored the response, it's that old response that comes forward anytime a situation in adulthood has the same flavor.

We won't necessarily *consciously* recognize that this triggering event is bringing up a childhood response, but we can notice the clues when our adult brain goes offline, our emotions escalate, and our reactions are untempered.

In fact, we are never upset for the reason we think we are.

When we are experiencing peaked emotions and are inside a triggered response, then we are reacting *to our past*, not our present. If we are to be fair about the situation, maybe only 10 percent of what is happening right in front of us is actually the problem, and 90 percent (or more!) is what is happening *inside of us*. And what is happening inside of us is that our preset neural pathways have been triggered and our unconscious is reliving the initial experience, only as an adult in the present moment.

If you've ever wondered why the person you are arguing with is behaving like a child, well, in some sense, they actually are!

While this sounds like entrapment by the unconscious, it's

actually the soul's opportunity to heal. If in that moment of triggering, rather than reinforcing that deep, old childhood neural pathway, *we are shown* something different, then we have a golden opportunity to flip that script, react differently to the situation, release the trauma, and heal the wound. If, in that moment, our partner reveals trustworthiness, compassion, love — something different than what we expect — then we get to see our world (and our partner) differently. We drop the emotional reactivity, and our neural pathway, our inner truth, gets rewritten. Instead of thinking of the universe as hostile, we view it as friendly. And we realize the extraordinary value of intimate connection.

We are healed through relationship.

The profound irony about this process is that it is through relationship that we are originally wounded, and it is through relationship that we are ultimately restored. Inevitably, that first relationship with our parents or caregivers sets up the initial wounding in the psyche, and then we play this out by projecting that wound onto our relationships throughout our life, until we find a worthy companion who both mirrors our childhood experience and loves us enough to help us slay our inner demons. Through the right partnership, we test the limits of our inner truths and discover what has been buried all along: our potential, our fullness, our connection with others, and our deep satisfaction with life and ourselves.

6

The Satisfied Relationship

Perhaps the most important relationship for the modern adult feminine woman is intimate partnership. Far from being a clichéd or old-fashioned notion, it is within the sacred dynamic of masculine and feminine that the feminine flourishes. This relationship has the potential to heal the greatest wounds suffered by the feminine, which are often — ironically — at the hands of the distorted masculine.

Whether it was our father, brother, boys at school, or members of our wider community, it is nearly inevitable that a young woman experiences some type of psychological, emotional, or physical harm from the opposite polarity. Whether unintentional or intended, whether violent or subtle, these leave indelible marks on the psyche that forever shape our adulthood.

Part of the power of being an adult woman is having the opportunity to heal these wounds and behave differently to teach not only our daughters but also our sons a different way to treat the feminine. This healing happens through our intimate relationships.

I can't emphasize it enough: We are wounded in relationship. And we are ultimately healed in relationship.

While therapy can play a role in this healing, and we certainly benefit from therapeutic practices in order to resolve all types of trauma, in the end therapeutic work is enlivened, emboldened, and ingrained in our psyche through positive interactions with intimate partners. We must come to fully understand what it connotes to be the feminine in partnership with the masculine and how to use that relationship as a key to our feminine soul's healing.

It is possible, especially with the right counterpart. But it requires a reframing of what we may have learned early on about what it means to be a woman in relationship, as well as a new understanding of the masculine we choose to partner with. Like a secret formula, the right dynamic between the masculine and the feminine creates an alchemy that transforms proverbial lead into gold. When the mix of vulnerability, connection, engagement, commitment, trust, and willingness is just right, the opposite polarities interact to produce a glorious result: a relationship that catalyzes the best in both people.

We traditionally think of alchemy as the practice of mixing unstable concoctions to produce unpredictable yet magical results. Stories are told of wild alchemists, just on the edge of towns, casually blowing up their laboratories in pursuit of the right mixture to produce the magnum opus, the great work: the philosopher's stone. Alchemy was as much a literal pursuit of impossible chemistry to create gold from lead as it was a mindset, a philosophy, a psychology — a way of life. The alchemists held many things sacred, including the oppositional forces of the universe, the masculine and the feminine, which were often represented as the sun (masculine) and the moon (feminine). Alchemical artwork and literature speak of the conjunction of these two as the most heralded result of alchemy, giving rise to the ultimate result that they called "the philosopher's stone": self-knowledge. The philosopher's stone was not a literal gem, but a metaphorical one, meant to represent an understanding, not of the external world, but of the more precious internal one: the landscape of your own psyche and soul.

As the alchemists say: "As above, so below."

Just like the medieval alchemists who tinkered with chemicals to experiment with new mixtures, we engage in relational alchemy when we are in an intimate partnership. We are seeking the right chemistry between two individuals to produce our own sacred result: harmony between the polarities. This harmony does not negate or flatten the polarities. It doesn't render them depolarized, but rather utilizes the most spectacular features of each in order to produce a third thing — the most sacred thing. Between two people, that third thing is not the opus of the philosopher's stone. Instead, that third thing, that opus, is *the relationship itself.*

If we think of a relationship as its own entity, as a thing that functions outside of and simultaneously between two people, then we each as individuals are free to contribute to that relationship in our own unique way. Of course, it is what we contribute that determines the quality of the relationship, the preciousness of the opus.

If we contribute our fears, hang-ups, cynicism, resentment, and jealousy, then what flavor does the relationship opus take? Is it a stable chemical balance? Or does it explode like the volatile alchemical huts of old?

What if, instead, we protect and cherish the relationship as the greatest gift we can create? What if we contribute our dreams, hopes, commitment, trust, creativity, providership, cherishing, adoration, kindness, generosity, forgiveness — all that we wish to draw from and thrive off forevermore? What kind of relationship opus do we create then?

An opus that is true gold.

According to alchemy, to create the opus, there must be a mixture of opposites — literally referred to as a "chemical wedding." This marriage of oppositional forces sometimes creates sparks. Make it too volatile, and the laboratory explodes, with no resulting opus. Too little interaction between the chemicals, and there is insufficient energy for fusion. We need just enough spark — chemistry — to produce a bond that not only preserves the integrity of the original elements but also completely transforms them into something new and more valuable.

Alchemy is dead sexy.

It presents a perfect metaphorical recipe for intimacy between opposite polarities. The alchemists of old understood relationship dynamics and how precise they needed to be with their mixtures. They knew that experimentation was required to find just the right mix for just the right result. We do this in our lives today when we engage in intimate relationship with the opposite polarity, too.

We try mixing with different people to determine the results. With some people, we clash right away, producing too much spark, causing an explosion. With others, we mix and dilute so much that all energy is lost. And with the precious one (or few) who stands the test of time and whose chemistry, by mixing with ours, produces gold? Well, then, we have found the precious opus.

What we must keep in mind is that to really test this opus, we need to see not only how the relationship transforms through the alchemical mixture, but *how we are transformed by it.* The right opus — the third thing, that relationship between the two — is not only a transformation, but *transformational.* It uses its own energy to burn off what is no longer required to sustain the alchemical gold.

Through the chemical wedding, we are able to release the dross of our psyche and let go of what doesn't serve the gold of the opus. It is the energy — the heat, the spark — of this alchemical process that refines all three elements: the masculine, the feminine, and the relationship opus between them. Under the right circumstances, it is nothing short of a magical process.

Which is why it is worth seeking out the right circumstances.

No matter the external shape an intimate relationship takes — long-term, short-term, dating, cohabitating, any iteration you choose — you know that it is right for you when it creates this alchemical transformation. When you discover the opus, the gold, as a result of mixing with another human, then you know you have found something precious and worth digging into. It won't be without its heat, fire, challenge, or occasional unstable reaction, but ultimately these challenges are worth it as long as the gold keeps shining. This is a precious gift and a source of tremendous satisfaction — for the feminine, the masculine, and the relationship itself.

The Case for Companionship

Pursuing relationship gold is a lifetime process. There may be one perfect mix that results in your opus, or there may be many iterations — whatever balance you strike is determined by whatever part of your personal journey you are on. Sometimes, that road is walked alone.

Because of our culture's current values of independence and individuality, as well as various other modern societal factors, many women are solo — perhaps more than at any other time in history. Whether it is due to personal preference, or because she hasn't found a suitable masculine counterpart (ladies, I don't envy *anyone* on the dating scene these days!), or because of a recent breakup, or because family members have left the home, it is very possible that a woman is alone at some point in her life. This is unique to our contemporary culture, because historically it is a very new condition for women.

Throughout history, human beings have lived in collaborative, cohabitative environments. We have always been tribal, living in close proximity to other family and tribe members, and there are very good reasons for this. We are the only species whose young can't fend for themselves shortly after birth and who require so much support even after the point at which we can feed ourselves. Children of the tribe require not just parenting but grandparenting and neighboring to reach beyond the many awkward years of childhood to become functioning adult members of the tribe. Essentially, it took the village to raise one another up, keep one another safe, and ensure the survival of all members of the tribe.

Over time, we evolved to require close relationships to other humans not just for survival purposes but also for our overall mental health and well-being.

We humans are hardwired for connection. Our very existence depends on empathic connections to others. It is empathy that has kept tribes alive since time immemorial. Empathic connection gives us purpose, direction, collaboration, and motivation — all things that help humans thrive as a species. When we offer kindness, compassion, and love to others, we create mutually beneficial environments that provide safety, security, and trust, as well as ensure that our most important relations have everything they need.

We need one another. Full stop.

Living alone is an unnatural state for a human. It means that the safety, security, and resources otherwise provided by tribe members all fall on the one human to provide for herself. This creates a level of stress that our foremothers would never have encountered and could not have overcome, as women historically were not allowed to work or engage in certain other activities that would have helped ensure survival. Today, we are able to work and provide for ourselves, we are able to sign a lease or buy a house, we are able to lock the doors and install security systems, and we are able to stream TV shows for company... but it still doesn't meet the needs of our psyche and soul if we do this only for ourselves and all by ourselves all the time. For the feminine woman, tending to all our own needs — whether they are emotional, psychological, spiritual, or physical — is an exhausting process.

In perpetual aloneness, the feminine woman must hold both the masculine and the feminine polarities for herself. In a masculine-dominated, patriarchal culture, this means that the demands of her masculine side are great. She needs to elevate her logical mind, protect herself from the world, and lead herself on a path to success. Women can do all these things, *of course*. But in providing all the masculine support for herself, the modern woman may find it *very* difficult to downshift out of that masculine mode long enough to elevate her femininity and allow it to flourish. When the demands of her independent life drive her to succeed on a man's terms, it is easy to lose the ability to surrender to her feminine side and foster the receptivity, creativity, joy, and pleasure she can find therein. When the expectations of being able to do everything herself means she manhandles her whole world, it becomes difficult to receive anything (help, connection, resources) from anyone else.

Independence and individualism are highly valued in our culture. One of the greatest pieces of advice I received as a young woman was that it is important to live alone, at least for a short time, to build the confidence that you can take care of yourself under any circumstances. Life is not easy to live (as my grandma would say). For women who have never affirmed their independence, suddenly being alone can be debilitating. I witnessed the difficulty of a close friend trying to find her footing in her sixties, when her spouse of thirty years died and she had never lived solo or paid her own bills. Alone sometimes happens, and sometimes it is a choice. However, as a permanent strategy for the feminine, I don't recommend it.

While it's incredibly valuable and empowering for women to have complete confidence that they can handle every inch of their lives (security, safety, finances, relationships, family, spirituality, et cetera), it's even more valuable for a woman to know what she wants to own in her life as the feminine polarity. Then she can cultivate circumstances for her femininity to flourish with the support of others, including a worthy intimate partner when the time and person are right for her.

The psychological reality of human nature means that intimate relationships are required for our utmost health and well-being. They just are. I know many of us swear off intimate relationships after one ends because of the hurt associated with that experience. I get it. I was raised by a mother who pledged she would never again deal with men and intimate relationships after a very traumatic divorce. I've seen friends vow up and down that they were done with relationships after horrible breakups, infidelity, even abuse.

Do you know what happens to these women?

They end up back in relationships.

This isn't a fatal flaw. This isn't outside of integrity. This is simply human. Relationship is inherent to our basic programming. We are built to love, commiserate, and relate. Intimacy is not just a birthright, it's a basic human need. It's a feature of our evolutionary survival instincts.

The mirror neurons in our brain fire when we see the emotional expressions of people around us, and mirror neurons are the biological trigger for the feeling of empathy. Mirror neurons help us connect with others and feel seen by others. The summation is that they developed as a result of our tribal nature and that our survival actually depends on collaboration with our tribe. We come together to love one another, support one another, guarantee each other's survival, and fight common enemies.

Essentially, there is only so far we can go solo in our emotional and psychological development. We need the powerful reflection — the activation of the mirror neurons — to spark the range of emotions and deep psychological truths buried within the psyche. Intimate relationship allows us to achieve the deepest levels of emotional reflection with another human. While our family relationships and friendships spark emotion and kindle our unconscious, nothing touches what is buried within us quite like intimate relationship.

So try as we might for as long as we can, inevitably intimacy creeps back into our lives. It's not a great mystery as to why, and it is not a great detriment, either. Intimate partnership does not signal weakness or an inability to take care of ourselves. Establishing healthy intimate relationships fosters an interdependence with another that is encoded into our evolution as humans.

Being interdependent doesn't remove our individualism or even necessarily our independence. Having the support of the opposite polarity in intimate relationship actually allows us to thrive in our primary polarity and lean more fully into our gifts. If we are trying to provide all things at all times to ourself, something is sacrificed in that compromise. In today's world, it is usually our femininity that gets lost... and everyone suffers from the imbalance.

Now, while the importance of having intimate partnership in our life cannot be overlooked or underestimated, what I'm *not* advocating here is any sort of magical thinking, like "calling the right man in" or asserting that we have to hunt down our only "soulmate" on the planet. I'm also not saying that a woman "needs" a man 100 percent of the time. These types of tropes are terribly disempowering and destabilizing for the feminine. I've seen too many books on the bestseller list trying to teach a woman how to contort herself into her "perfect" partner's ideals in order to enchant him to her doorstep or how to "be more feminine" to attract "the one."

Stop it. Just. Stop.

Before I dive into what the Satisfied Woman needs in the masculine intimate partner she chooses, let me be clear on what she doesn't need. She doesn't need to give any of herself up or away. She doesn't need to retrofit herself into some vintage ideal of womanhood, barefoot and pregnant in the kitchen, serving dinner at five, and maintaining silence at the table. She doesn't need to abdicate her desires in favor of what she is told to do. And she certainly doesn't need a masculine partner who doesn't support her needs, cherish her, or make decisions with her highest good in mind.

The Satisfied Woman's intimate relationship can look like whatever she damn well wants, so long as it enhances the Four Keys in her life: safety, security, and her ability to trust and be cherished. She can choose one partner or several over her lifetime. There may be one who serves her highest good at one time and another at a different time. I'm not here to structure (or judge!) the types of relationships available to women today. What I am here to suggest is that they need to *feel good* and *support your highest good* as a feminine woman.

Intimate partnership unlocks the feminine energy within us and gives us a foundation from which to thrive. Allowing a masculine partner to take the lead (if only on the dance floor), provide us with protection (if only by giving us his raincoat), and contribute to our well-being (if only by providing a shoulder when we cry) is critical...but it must be *on our terms and when we desire it*. Forget the imbalanced relationships of our foremothers. We are lucky that we can structure our partnerships in the way that works best for us. But let that structure be built on the foundation of the Four Keys. That is how you can be certain it will satisfy the feminine.

Finding the Right (Counter)Partner

Perhaps the most important consideration for the feminine woman when she is searching for the right partner is finding someone on the opposite polarity. This may sound trivial — especially at this stage of the book — but you would be surprised at how people both misunderstand and misrepresent their polarity. I can't tell you how often I have spoken to people about the dynamics of the masculine and feminine and piqued their interest, only to have them discover that they are *not* on the polarity they thought they were. Or that they've spent so much time on the wrong polarity that they are misrepresenting themselves and ultimately attracting the wrong kind of partner as a result.

The good news is that to determine whether or not you (or a potential mate) are on the right polarity, you need only ask one question.

This is an easy question to ask. And answer.

It is easy because your psyche and soul already know which polarity is dominant within you. Remember, we all have both! But each of us desires to lean into one more than the other more often. And, perhaps most importantly, each of us desires to be known most completely in terms of one polarity or the other.

That being said, the only question — in fact, the Key Question — you need to ask to determine which polarity is dominant for you is this: In intimate relationship, do you prefer to be respected? Or cherished? This Key Question is foundational in determining the primary polarity of yourself, your intimate partners, and anyone else around you. By asking it early and often, you understand more clearly the oppositional playing field each of you is on!

The answer that comes to you first is correct for you. No need to second-guess yourself or overly apply logic to your response. No need to justify the reply that appears quickly. Simply honor the thought that arises. It comes from a soul level and is the best one for you at this time.

If you know you need to be respected, then your primary polarity is the masculine.

If your instinct is to be cherished, then your primary polarity is the feminine.

The healthy masculine desires to be respected from a place of love, not blind acquiescence. The feminine respects his decisions because she knows he is acting in her/their highest good. And the feminine desires to be cherished by an openhearted, loving masculine who prioritizes her emotions and intuitive needs above his own — even if doing so makes him uncomfortable or doesn't feel "logical" to him. He understands that her deep desire for safety and security are what prompt her intuitive insights and emotions, and he does what he can to cherish them and meet her needs.

When we find this energetic balance between masculine and feminine, each person is able to fully embrace and settle into their natural polarity. It is in this partnership that we are free to explore and pursue the relationship opus.

Stages of Relationship

True feminine satisfaction is the pleasure derived from the fulfillment of our needs, and as we've seen, the foundation of such

satisfaction lies in establishing the Four Keys in our life: safety, security, and the ability to trust and be cherished. While the Four
Keys are critical in every area — social, professional, familial, spiritual, and psychological — they are perhaps most important in intimate relationship.

While this is not a book about magnetizing your "soulmate,"
nor do I harp on the importance of finding "the one," it is true that
at some point in our lives we all engage in intimate partnership,
and it is also true (from a psychological perspective) that the greatest healing comes through relationship.

Intimate relationships are extremely important.

And whether we have one or many, whether they are short- or
long-term, whether we want one at this moment or not, it is
important to know how to navigate them in a way that establishes
the Four Keys and lays the groundwork for creativity, passion, joy,
and enthusiasm. We need to thrive, transform, heal, and recharge
through relationship. It is how we discover the innermost workings of our soul. Yes, we can do some of this alone. But we can
never take ourselves as far on the personal journey as we can with
an intimate partner.

I can't say it enough: intimate partnership has the potential to
yield alchemical gold.

Just like in the alchemical practices of the past, in relationship
there is a well-worn process for optimizing the chances of success. While the alchemists' concoctions didn't always result in the
golden opus — and not all our relationships will either — there
are some foundational principles that help make that success more
likely. Satisfaction is possible when we understand what to look for
in relationship and what to cultivate.

Might as well know what we are in for, right? After all, knowledge is power. If we enter a relationship not just with rose-colored
glasses (because let's be honest, that first phase is fun) but also
with our beakers and mixing tools at the ready, we are much more
prepared for the journey.

And make no mistake, relationship is a journey. You want to

find the ideal partner, the one with the best attitude and skills to help you on the path. It's a path you walk together, and even in the places where you must journey alone, you still keep a lifeline connected to the other. This isn't a path to tread lightly; you need to approach it with deadly seriousness so you don't get caught in traps along the way. An intimate relationship is as much the outward journey the two of you embark on as it is the inward journey that each of you traverses individually, but with the support of the other. It's perhaps the most important journey that any of us endeavors in our lifetimes.

No matter how you meet someone, it is typically chemistry that draws you to them. We have all felt it. We all know it. It is that je ne sais quoi of attraction that brings you into another person's orbit. In alchemy, a spark is required between the oppositional substances if there is ever to be any hope of producing the opus. It is the same between two people! I wish we had a perfect formula to predict which two individuals will be able to produce relationship gold, but just like unpredictable alchemical substances, we humans can be unstable and variable and subject to our external conditions. Only on taking our chances with the mix do we find out whether two elements come together well. The *prima materia* — the initial matter — that each of us brings into a relationship includes all our personal history, assumptions, experiences, knowledge, projections, and expectations. The full contents of the *prima materia* tend to be revealed over time.

In the first stage of relationship, we see through the haze of all our assumptions and expectations. Often referred to as seeing through rose-colored glasses, it is more accurately described as a not-yet-knowing of the other person. We see mostly ourselves. And we see in them only what we wish to see (known as a *projection*). This is made even more challenging by the chemical reaction created with the mix, what is called *nigredo* in alchemy. For us humans, this chemical reaction takes the form of reactive hormones flooding the body for the first six to twelve months of a relationship. Yep, there are actual chemical reactions that occur as a result of interpersonal chemistry! The other person's physical touch ignites the oxytocin receptors on the skin, saturating our system with feelings of adoration. The delight of intimacy creates an uptick in dopamine and serotonin, which makes us feel good about ourself and life in general. With these addictive hormones coursing through our bodies, it's no wonder we overlook idiosyncratic behaviors that would normally drive us nuts. We happily don the rose-colored glasses, which show us more of what we want to see than what is actually in front of us.

For this reason, it tends to be much easier to start a new relationship and much, much harder to stay in one. Eventually, the hormones wane, the rose-colored glasses come off, and we do see the problematic behaviors. What initially came off as exciting feels compromising. What was once endearing becomes annoying. What seemed chivalrous feels chauvinistic. This is when we are more accurately able to learn who it is we are dealing with — and when the real work of relationship begins.

Because everyone is human. And as we have learned, everyone has a deep, unconscious wellspring of personal truths, assumptions, and triggers that eventually see the light of day inside intimate partnership. While nearly everything is overcome-able, fundamentally we need to be dealing with a person who is *as interested in overcoming the impossible and healing their psyche as we are*. We need to be dealing with a person willing to do their best to always lean toward the light.

As one of my good friends likes to say, anyone can be an excellent partner for six to twelve months — because our body's chemicals help us project the best qualities onto our partner while overlooking their fatal flaws. As a result, we sometimes end up painting red flags green.

In the initial *nigredo* state, we are still very much in the dark about our partner's true nature, because the chemical reactions haven't allowed us to see it yet. And while we are gathering information, experiences, and knowledge about our partner in this initial phase, until those chemicals dissipate, it is difficult to understand if the chemical reaction between you is productively volatile or a dud. However, the beauty of the *nigredo* phase is that it is usually delightful and exciting. It provides an opportunity to lay down the initial groundwork of shared experience that can carry you through the next phases of the relationship — should this coupling prove to be worthy of continued exploration!

No matter how many sparks are flying at the beginning, it is wise to maintain healthy boundaries around your femininity and your most important needs. Keep the Four Keys in mind as you do your best to witness the behavior of your partner. See how they react, respond, and treat you when you voice a need or voice your intuition. There are some boundaries that should never be crossed. Some red flags that should never be painted green. You determine what those are for yourself on the basis of your ability to feel safe, to feel secure, to trust your partner, and to be cherished by them. Let your intuition guide you regarding any feelings of discomfort that arise, and if you are not properly heard and acknowledged when you voice your needs, it is time to take the rose-colored glasses off.

Inevitably, the flood of hormones wanes, and we return from the land of limerence back to reality. While the *nigredo* phase ignites the chemistry, the next phase, *albedo*, is where the real work begins. This is the clarifying phase where we emerge from the hazy darkness of the chemical overload and are back into our fully emotionally regulated and more rational adult psyche. This is when we see if the relationship is stable enough to work the *prima materia* with enough heat to create the third thing — that relationship opus.

We decide during this second stage whether the relationship is ultimately worth a continued investment. Without the spark of the first stage, we may tire of the idiosyncrasies we once thought were adorable. We may start to question behavior we once overlooked. We may see through the ruse of avoidance and realize we are not on the same page with the other person. Typically, it is in the *albedo* that the rose-colored glasses come off and the fighting gloves go on. It may even feel like we are now in a relationship with a whole different person.

In reality, we are actually no longer seeing our projections — we are finally seeing the other person. This is when we really get to know our intimate partner. And this is when we create that sacred third thing between two people: the relationship opus. We start to put into the relationship all that makes it sacred...or all that makes it toxic. If we can't get past our own projections or expectations, then the other person continues to disappoint us. If we put our fears, worries, misgivings, doubts, or dissatisfactions into the relationship, the opus degrades and is doomed to fail.

However, after that initial spark, with the fullness of intention and desire to invest in the relationship itself, two people can come together not only to create something beautiful between them but also to create transformation and beauty within themselves. In the *albedo* phase is when we realize we are projecting onto the other instead of seeing them fully; we clean up our own shadow so that we can know the relationship as it *is* rather than as we *expect* it to be. After all, expectations are simply premeditated disappointments. And as long as we continue to project our expectations on another person, we never allow them to reveal themselves.

We need to release our expectations and let go of our projections in order to let our partner invest themselves fully in the relationship. We need to give the best of ourselves to creating the relationship opus. We infuse the relationship opus with our wishes, inspirations, kindness, compassion, trust, commitment — all the things we want our relationship to be built on. In this way, the relationship becomes your support system. Your lifeline. The litmus test by which you pass everything in your life — every decision, every desire, every hope, every dream.

Let me be clear: *It is the relationship that is the container.* Not the other person.

When both people are focused on self-development for the purpose of propagating the gold between them, that is the opus. When both people invest in positive affirmations toward the other to cultivate more joy, that is the opus. When each individual refrains from divesting their energy and attention elsewhere and instead always turns *toward* the relationship, that is the opus.

It is about two people coming together to create something nourishing and sustaining between them.

We know it's a healthy relationship when each individual is thriving in their primary polarity, respected and cherished for who they are, and when the relationship is *additive* to their fullest expression of life. There is no detriment or diminution to the individuals, and it is not about creating a toxic dependence or codependence.

The ultimate relationship opus offers you the ability to continuously examine yourself in order to reveal more of what is in your own soul. Proper relationship reveals this to us by inevitably bringing up our deepest emotions and pulling our most sensitive triggers. Rather than flounder, an invested partner shows us a *different* reaction than we expect, which helps to change the patterning in our psyche and ultimately sets us free from the pain and suffering encoded within us.

Just like the process of alchemy, an alchemically inspired relationship promotes change and helps us transform our inner darkness into light. In the right relationship, this process fosters trust. When we trust our partner to have our best interest at heart, we trust ourselves to be vulnerable and use the container of the relationship for inner transformation.

It is often said that trust is not given — it is earned. It is earned when one partner turns toward the other to support and work through triggers and challenges. There is no way to avoid conflict between two people. Conflict is the continued spark of the psychological process providing substance for the alembic of alchemical change. It is not something to be avoided, but it is something that needs to be processed…together. When we trust our partner to turn toward us during conflict and remain in integrity with their words and actions as we resolve our differences, the relationship deepens and trust is strengthened.

Conflict during this stage — when we are just getting to know the actual human we are in relationship with — is hard. We don't yet have enough of a track record to be able to predict how conflict will end. We are not certain if conflict will escalate and result in eruption, rejection, avoidance, or worse. Staying in the transformative fire with the other person and *witnessing* how they handle the heat time and time again is what ultimately builds trust between you.

As Oprah says Maya Angelou once told her, "When people show you who they are, believe them."

Because your intimate partner may be amazing when things are going great, but they could reveal something different in conflict. Maybe they make you coffee in the morning or shower you with compliments as you jet off to work, only to lose their cool at the towels being left on the floor or berate you for spending habits they don't agree with. It is the moments of tension, upset, or transgression that reveal the contents of their psyche and soul.

And — perhaps counterintuitively — it is within the conflict that trust is built. When no matter what happens between you, your partner maintains your sense of safety and security, when they cherish you even in heated moments, that's when you know you can trust them.

Once you have developed trust in the *albedo* stage by learning how you and your intimate partner weather the spark of conflict, you finally land in the phase of commitment. The final step of the process, after all the heat has been applied, is called the *rubedo*, which produces the glowing golden opus that is the mark of healthy, supportive relationship. The *rubedo* comes from the mixing of two opposites — masculine and feminine — that reveals the *coniunctio*, or the conjunction, which is the pinnacle of alchemy, namely, the aforementioned magnum opus or the philosopher's stone. This is the same thing that psychologists call individuation and the mystics call enlightenment. The important distinction here is that it cannot be reached alone, but rather only through relationship with our counterpart.

The *rubedo* stage is when we know our relationship is bulletproof and will withstand all outside forces. The relationship opus is solid, indestructible; we demonstrate our faith in it through our level of commitment. In this day and age, a fully committed partnership can be defined in many ways. Some partners desire marriage as a level of commitment; some are comfortable with cohabitation; others are fine with living apart but being in constant communication. The definition of commitment comes from the two partners and needs to rise to the level of comfort defined by each person. But no matter the demonstration of commitment, it always has one salient quality: each partner *actively chooses the relationship*. Every. Single. Day.

That is commitment.

Imagine that everywhere you and your intimate partner go, everything you do — whether separately or together — you do with the mindset of benefiting the relationship. Consider how you might behave at the gym with your partner in mind or in the conversations you have with friends. When you and your intimate partner prioritize the relationship, that is commitment. Prioritizing the relationship means that no one throws the other under the bus or engages in emotional infidelity. Decisions are made for the highest good of the relationship, whether they be about finances, morals, ethics, behavior, scheduling, friendships, career — you name it.

When both people are deeply invested in keeping the gold shining in the relationship opus, there is no question of priorities. Ultimately, what benefits the relationship benefits each individual, too. It is an additive, restorative, healing experience that enhances the lives of both partners. The *rubedo* phase is where relationships truly thrive. When you have trust and loyalty as the foundations, it becomes possible to weather any storms that come along, including ones that happen between you.

Relationships are always work, but the right ones are worth it. When the work happens both outside and inside to reveal the best of both partners, then you have truly struck gold.

Getting Needs Met

Over the years, I've taken to asking long-term couples about their recipe for success. With couples who have been married for decades, I figure they have had enough time and practice to offer some helpful words of advice. I've received answers you may have guessed: "Never go to bed mad." "Resort to humor when possible." And so forth. But the most important piece of advice from a couple happily married more than sixty years was this: "Always help each other get your needs met."

This one stuck with me.

It was a stunning insight into the nature of intimacy and the importance of respecting and cherishing one another. Humans who don't have needs met are unhappy, and who would ever want their beloved partner to be unhappy?

What is the point of an intimate relationship if it doesn't enhance well-being, happiness, pleasure, joy, and all the good things in life that we so desire? And conversely, what if the relationship doesn't support the most basic needs we have?

I cannot overstate this point: *getting your needs met is the most important common element of intimate relationship.* If both partners are not fully invested in doing what they can to help meet each other's needs, then the relationship alchemy inevitably fails. Whatever values you prioritize in relationship, whatever has brought you together, whatever quirks each of you adore about the other, if you are not both willing to devote yourselves to the needs of the other, then this is not a relationship.

It is a sinking ship.

No one needs to stay on a sinking ship.

When we are with the right intimate partner, their investment in meeting our needs matches our own investment in meeting theirs. It's the thing we do to contribute to the relationship, to make that sacred third thing — the relationship — a safe, secure, wonderful place to be.

It is an act of devotion, something that takes us outside of ourselves and our own selfish notions and makes life bigger. It connects us to another human being and grows our heart. The effects of this cannot be overestimated. When we devote ourselves to a worthy partner in this way, we elevate our own mental health and well-being. We alleviate apathy, heal disconnection, find a sense of purpose in our lives, and avoid tendencies toward narcissism and isolation. We contribute to the well-being of another, which lessens depression and anxiety.

In fact, people who are happy in their long-term committed relationships live longer, enjoy improved health, and have reduced stress. This is not true for unhappy relationships, nor is it true for people who live alone. Oddly, the best thing you can do for your health and longevity is to engage in a happy, mutually beneficial long-term committed partnership. Luckily, the key to creating a happy relationship is not rocket science.

It's meeting each other's needs.

Now, before we plunge down a rabbit hole of "buts" and "what ifs," let's assess all needs on the basis of whether they serve the highest good of both individuals in some way. If one partner's "need" feels damaging to the other or to the relationship, then it is a selfish request, not a need.

As long as needs fulfill the values of the relationship and serve the relationship, then each partner has a responsibility to help meet that need. Your partner may have a need for alone time or a weekend escape with friends. If it gives them the space and clarity to come back refreshed and happy to be in the relationship, then you would gladly help them get that need met. Or you may have a need for a dietary change or a sleep schedule shift. Though it might be uncomfortable, ultimately it could create better health for both of you, so by all means, your partner would want to meet that need. One partner may need to relocate for a job opportunity that advances their career, and even though it may mean leaving family and friends, if this helps you both reach the goals you have for the relationship, then it is probably time to start packing.

Meeting the needs that arise in the relationship may require some sacrifice. Sacrifice is part of the love you give to the other. It is the cost of buying into the relationship gold you create together. Everything of value is worthy of its price. And that energetic exchange you offer — the willingness to compromise — actually makes the relationship and your partner *more* valuable to you. It means you each have skin in the game. It means you each are choosing the relationship, day after day. It means you each are committed wholeheartedly to the partnership.

Of course, beware of needs that are harmful to the other or to the relationship. When a need subjugates, diminishes, or negates in any way, that results in manipulation and martyrdom. One partner manipulates the other into meeting their selfish request, while the other martyrs themself to honor the request. This is a foundational behavior of codependency, which never ends well. In the simplest terms, codependency occurs when someone is perceived as not having their own inner agency, and so they either need outside help or are subject to coercion. When someone is viewed as disempowered, incomplete, or in need of assistance only someone else can provide, then codependency kicks in.

In a codependent relationship, there are three roles: the rescuer, the persecutor, and the victim. The victim is always the disempowered person, the one viewed as not capable. In fact, a person may *play* the victim in order to solicit help and sympathy from another. We know someone is playing the victim when there is a sense of "poor me," or that the problems are the world's fault and not their own, or when they feel they have no agency in a situation. A victim pairs with a persecutor or a rescuer. A rescuer is effectively an enabler of bad behavior, the one who makes excuses for the victim, believes their inauthentic cries for help, or takes them back just one more time. "But they need me" is the sentiment of the rescuer, who believes that those around them are incapable of doing for themselves what needs to be done. A persecutor, on the other hand, blames, shames, and lashes out at the victim. The persecutor finds fault and criticizes the victim, leaving no room for mercy or an open heart. The persecutor always feels that they are absolutely right and that everyone else is wrong.

In codependency, people often switch among these three roles. The victim may get tired of the persecutor lashing out and so may become a persecutor themselves. The rescuer might be fed up with the victim's behavior and become a persecutor. Or a rescuer or persecutor may turn into a victim when they seek sympathy for all their attempts to change the other person. It's a vicious cycle. One that digs at the heart of our deepest and most lasting wounds in the unconscious. Codependency itself is an unconscious behavior that needs awareness and support to resolve. It is possible to elevate oneself out of codependency, but not as long as we believe we "need" another person or we believe they "need" us. Remember, meeting the needs of another never disempowers them or us, but rather elevates and adds to their well-being and ours.

Healthy relationships are not codependent. They are *interdependent*. Being in a relationship is not a source of weakness or an act of submission. It is not giving up, giving over, or giving in. A healthy relationship serves the highest good and seeks to meet the needs of the people in it. We are empowered, enlivened, and enthused through relationship. And when the relationship brings us pleasure from the fulfillment of our needs, it creates great satisfaction.

Being the Feminine in Relationship

Forget Mars and Venus! The masculine and feminine in alchemical terms are the sun (masculine) and the moon (feminine). And, as we've covered in this book so far, each of those polarities has salient qualities that make them unique and interdependent with the other. But as feminine women in today's world, we navigate a lot of masculinity and in fact often have to wear the mask of masculinity to get through our daily lives. When we are alone and independent, we move between the masculine and feminine to respond to the circumstances of daily life, but the reality of our patriarchal world means that we probably present more masculinity more often than we would like.

This creates quite a conundrum, because in order to find the masculine partner you seek, it is critical for you to be your feminine self. When they say that opposites attract, it is less about interests and more about the polarities that result in the attraction! The masculine is attracted to the feminine and vice versa. Just like magnets, opposite polarities are drawn toward each other, whereas the same poles repel each other. We can't expect to find the masculine partner of our dreams if we are perpetually occupying the masculine ourselves.

What are we to do, then, when we want to enter into an intimate partnership with the masculine? What happens when we desire to be the feminine counterpart and create a trusting, committed relationship full of sexy sparks? When we feel the urge to relax into our feminine nature with the support of a worthy masculine partner, how do we downshift out of all our own masculine tendencies?

Because the reality is that too much of one polarity in any intimate relationship results in a fizzle or a flop. When two people of the same polarity (regardless of gender) attempt to engage in intimacy, it feels like either you are dating your friend or you are dating your worst enemy. It is the opposition that generates the alchemical spark needed for relationship gold. This means that as the feminine counterpart, we must be ready and willing to remain in the feminine polarity while we are engaged in intimate relationship.

Don't take this the wrong way. In no manner does this mean that we subjugate ourselves, suddenly become passive, or forgo our own needs. It means, rather, that we finally get to drop the mask of masculinity when we are with a trusted, committed partner and fully express all the most glorious elements of our femininity. We lean into our intuition, we honor our emotional experience, we explore our creativity, we revel in pleasure and ecstasy whenever possible. It means we slide into the space of trusting our relationship and allowing ourselves to be cherished by the masculine.

It also means that we, as feminine women, respect our masculine partners. Particularly, we respect the decisions he makes. For the masculine, the freedom to make his own decisions and be respected for them is paramount to his sense of self. We know he's the right partner for us when those decisions he freely makes take our highest needs into account and benefit our relationship. When the decisions are *respectable*, it is easy to respect them. And when we find a masculine partner who cherishes us so much that his decisions are always in line with our highest good and he does his best to get our needs met, we have the potential to cultivate relationship gold.

However, if we remain in our masculine, there is no space for our masculine counterpart to thrive. He cannot show up for us in his masculinity if we constantly "manhandle" him or stay in the masculine ourselves. Just like the yin-yang symbol, the two polarities in opposition make the circle whole. We must embody and embrace our femininity in order to allow our partner to step up and into his masculinity. Otherwise, we run the risk of emasculating our partner and becoming burned out by inhabiting the wrong polarity ourselves.

I know this is tough to hear, especially in a day and age where women are often celebrated for their masculine qualities, achievements, and pursuits. And I also know it's a difficult thing to hear when culturally the feminine is still viewed as weak and disadvantaged. I understand the pride of women being able to be all things to all people and get all the jobs done. But at the end of the day, the hypermasculinity of that attitude never lets the feminine flourish in intimate relationship. Remember, a key quality of femininity is the ability to receive. And the right masculine partner cherishes you and generously contributes to your well-being.

In a healthy relationship with the masculine, you respect his decision-making because he has earned that respect by showing you his decisions are always made with the relationship's and your highest good in mind. As I said, the masculine needs to have the freedom to make his own decisions, but in the context of a relationship, that freedom always takes the relationship into account and prioritizes the needs of the relationship over any selfish wants. If a masculine partner isn't ready to shift his priorities out of his selfish wants, then you know he is not ready for true partnership. Selfishness in decision-making is a common trait of the masculine who has not advanced his psyche from adolescence to adulthood. Remember, women have the biological kick into adulthood with the onset of our period. For men, without a coming-of-age ritual or event, there is a danger that they might stay in childish thinking and expect that the world revolves around their needs.

However, the realized adult masculine is recognized for his power and agency through contribution, providership, and leadership. The confident masculine deeply desires to provide for the needs of his partner (and, if he has them, his children) and to lead the relationship through his self-assured decisions. As the feminine, we need to let the masculine lead in this way. Now, I know that for my fiercely independent females, reading that may rankle. I'm not advocating that you abdicate your agency and kowtow to whatever whim your man wants. What I am saying is that when you find a masculine partner who *truly* has your back and your best interests at heart, you can relax and *receive* the benefit of those interests! Let him take the lead in the relationship while you enjoy the results of all his good decisions! If you try to manhandle things, it tells him you've lost confidence in his direction, and then he truly loses his way.

There are so many other areas of life where you have to don the masculine mask. And there are plenty of other decisions that you are responsible for. In the fight for control inside intimate partnership, though, everyone loses. Once again, to be the feminine in partnership is to let the masculine lead, and when he does, your love leads him in the best direction: toward *you*. Remember, the definition of satisfaction is the pleasure we get through the fulfillment of our wishes and needs. A worthy masculine partner helps get your needs met and cherishes you. The masculine, in an alchemically sound relationship, *lets you relax into your femininity.*

7

Women Are Not the Bottomless Well

Women today are exhausted, overwhelmed, overworked, and undermined. It's a tough reality brought about by a toxic combination of patriarchy, distorted masculinity, and modern (especially American) society's elevation of the kind of do-it-yourself independence that crosses into isolation and loneliness. While I am certainly all for every woman being able to take care of herself, and I think it's incredibly important that every woman know that she is fully capable in all areas of her life, something is lost in the assertion that a woman should be all things for herself and *also* all things for all those around her at all times.

We see this in women who cultivate successful careers and come home after a long day to continued demands to provide all the nurturing her family needs. We see this in women who choose to live alone and try to provide solace, safety, and security for themselves by binge-watching Netflix endlessly while activating their Ring alarms. We see this in women who relentlessly provide all the support for themselves and those around them because they are expected to provide it. And we see this in women who isolate themselves from female friendships for fear of judgment, comparison, or competition.

It is not only impractical but inhuman for an individual to stand alone against the world, to try to be all things to all people all the time…including themselves. Humans, perhaps most especially feminine women, are hardwired for connection to others and are not meant to be solitary in their efforts. Historically, women were relegated to domestic life, but in more modern times, women have far more liberties and the right to choose much different lives for themselves. However, more equality and liberty should not equate simply to more work, greater expectations, and more isolation. Moreover, the high value placed on independence nowadays means that not only is it possible for a woman to do it all (of course she can!), but she is expected to do it all. That expectation is the distorted masculine ravaging the feminine and taking what it wants without generosity, consideration, or consent.

Women are not bottomless wells.

Like a well, women are the bearers of life energy, the divine water that nourishes themselves and others. This is the essence of femininity. It lives within us and flows from us as pleasure, joy, creativity, emotions, intuition — all the things that make us divinely feminine. And as with a well, that essence needs to be tended to, cherished, and kept safe. A well is typically fed from groundwater. It cannot be drained at a rate greater than that at which it is replenished; otherwise the well dries up. And if the well runs dry, the topsoil suffers cracks, erosion, drought, and worse — life around it dies.

Those responsible for a well must provide it with great care. They must cherish the life-giving nature of the well so that they never draw from it without giving back or leaving the well with the resources to reenergize itself. Wells are also not freely available for anyone who wishes to drink.

Wells are precious. Wells are sacred. Wells have extraordinary value. These things are true of all women, too. Contrary to long-held patriarchal belief systems, women are not required to give everything they have to feed the world. It is not in the nature of the feminine to output energy at unsustainable levels simply because society, culture, family, or a relationship says she should.

In fact, as we have seen, the very essence of the feminine is receptivity. Her domain is that of receiving, the power to be filled up by life. As she is filled with this essence, she has the ability to run pleasure and creativity through her body. When she does, those around her benefit from that pleasure and creativity in myriad ways. Perhaps creativity blossoms as artistic endeavors or as the procreative forces that produce life. The pleasure-filled feminine inspires cherishing from the masculine, who is so enamored of and filled with joy by her that he seeks to protect her at all costs. And the pleasure-filled feminine is free to commune — rather than compete — with other women to generate friendship, joy, and inspiration in one another. While it is through the feminine that pleasure and creativity are generated, it is not *from* the feminine that these things should be willfully taken.

There is a difference between ravaging and ravishing the feminine. When we, as women, are not fully supported by the Four Keys — safety, security, trust, cherishing — and not thriving in our feminine polarity, then the danger is that our live-giving, pleasure-filled, creativity-inspiring wells are drawn from more quickly than they are replenished. We are ravaged to the point of dehydration and degradation. The woman whose well is dry is overwhelmed, exhausted, and unable to open to pleasure and creativity without it feeling forced or coerced.

We've been there as women when we are urged to "just give a little bit more," being tapped for more resources than we have to give. Whether the exhaustion comes at the end of a day or the end of a decade, when the well runs dry it is not just the woman who suffers, but everyone who builds their life around her life-giving waters. When people are thirsty, they become desperate and sometimes even aggressive in their demands for water. Humans must slake their thirst. But temperance is needed by the tenders of the well. They must understand that for the well to meet their needs, they must also meet the needs of the well!

Moreover, women have the potential to be, not just a well, but an oasis. In order to transition from a well to an oasis, we need to both feed our femininity and allow those around us to do the same.

In other words, we need to get comfortable receiving.

The ability to receive is inherently feminine. Somewhere in our cultural history this quality became distorted, and women were wrongly led to believe that we are the givers — the providers — of all things to all people. Instead, providership is the province of the masculine. It is enlivening to the masculine to lovingly offer whatever might be most supportive to those around them. And, in turn, it is enthusing and enamoring for the feminine to receive what is generously given. This is the exchange that provides the most nourishing access to the life-giving waters of the feminine. Everyone benefits, and she is so filled and fulfilled that she transforms into a beautiful oasis.

Interestingly, the word *oasis* comes from the Greek and Egyptian, meaning "dwelling place." This is a place of living, of rooting down, and of receiving what you need. An oasis is a home within the uninhabitable, a place of refuge, of joy, and of companionship.

Don't we all want to be near an oasis? Don't you want to be an oasis for others?

One of the traps we fall into in the distorted feminine viewpoint fostered by the patriarchal culture is that if we don't give freely of ourselves — drain ourselves — then people will abandon us. If we are not "enough," then we are not worthy of the generosity, love, or acceptance of others. It's a destructive feedback loop. What if instead of draining ourselves, we lived as if we were an oasis?

What if we stopped giving ourselves away?

As we overcontribute to our relationships, families, friendships, workplaces, and communities, we actually remove others' ability to step in. If we do everything for everyone, when do they actually do things for themselves? If we always do the laundry for the children, how do they learn to separate whites from colors? If we constantly tend to the emotional needs of our significant others, when do they console us in turn? If we're the one perpetually planning the girls' night out for our friends, how do they demonstrate their commitment to the friendship? If our work team is lagging on a project and we finish the job ourselves before the deadline, how do we empower the team to rise to the occasion and stretch their skills?

Here's my proposal: do less.

I know this idea is going to be a source of discomfort. I can hear the protests now: "But then the laundry won't get done!" Correct. It probably won't. For a while. Until they discover their deep need for those pants that have been lying on the floor for weeks. "But my significant other can't be expected to self-soothe!" Even babies learn to do this. I'm sure they will manage. "But there will never be another girls' night!" Don't worry, your girls will be itching to go out, and you'll get the call soon enough. "But the work will be late!" Most likely. But your boss knows who you are, and the team is now on notice to step up in the future.

Do less. For a while, even make yourself uncomfortable doing less. Feel that vacuum that appears when you stop overachieving and overcompensating.

And see what happens.

The universe hates a vacuum. Something always fills the void. And that's what fills up the well, allowing you to transform into an oasis.

With that extra life-giving energy you're preserving, you can finally tend to your own needs. Imagine having the space to take a movement class you have been wanting to try. Think of having the time to read the book you bought three years ago. What would it be like to spend an afternoon basking in the sunshine with a beloved friend? Move the activities that feed your soul from the back burner to the front. Let them reclaim their importance in your life and become the priority in your day.

The people around you will thank you for it. Trust me.

Watch as they notice your stress relief. Feel how the vibes around the house chill out, the tension around the workplace relaxes, the anxiety inside you begins to dissipate. In fact, as you nourish yourself by tending to your feminine needs and your well fills up, the people who love you *will want you to do more of it*. They see that these actions contribute to *your well…*being. They support you taking care of yourself, because they know that in the long run, they benefit from it, too. More than likely, they will come to value it even more than all your previous overachieving output. They step up to protect your most valuable resources: your feminine energy, emotions, and intuition. When you find the people who nurture you and who are easy and fulfilling to be around, keep them close and allow them to be dwellers around your oasis.

As for the people who continue to try to drain the well before it is replenished, decisions must be made, and boundaries must be drawn. They take more than they give. They expect more than they cherish. They ravage rather than ravish. They are easy to identify. In their presence you feel exhausted or ill at ease. You may have the urge to protect your time, energy, or resources and withhold any or all of those things in order to preserve yourself, which ultimately increases the tension between you. You walk away from their company quite literally feeling drained, and unless you engage in some serious downregulation of your nervous system and replenish your resources, that drain on your system translates to higher stress (read: cortisol) levels and negative health consequences (diminished immune response, disturbed sleep, anxiety, and more). These are the people around whom we need to draw protective boundaries of time and proximity. It may even be necessary to vote them off our island oasis. The opportunity to gather around our well and be in our life is a privilege, not a right. Feel free to revoke it when necessary!

For the people pleaser in us, this may sound like harsh medicine. How can we simply excise someone from our life who really needs us? It's one thing for others to need what we have to *offer*. It's a much different thing for others to ungratefully take what they extract from us through demands or expectations. Those drainers do not make themselves worthy of our gifts, whether they "need" them or not.

There is also, of course, the flip side of this double-edged sword. Martyrdom is the overwillingness to offer one's gifts to the point of depletion for the purpose of pleasing those around us. Unfortunately, martyrdom has the opposite effect: the recipients do not cherish what they receive, as they take us for granted. It's time to conserve our energy by stopping the martyrdom.

Even so, the presence of some people in our lives might be nonnegotiable. You may be related to them. They may live in your house. There are myriad reasons why it might be impossible to re-move someone from our oasis. While we must be discerning about all the relationships we do have a say in, for those that are unsever-able, we can still find strategies to manage our energy and mitigate the drain. It's all about drawing strong, impenetrable boundaries around our time and proximity to them and being fiercely protec-tive of our most precious resource: our feminine energy.

The Greek goddess Athena has much to teach us about this! While it might seem confusing to see a feminine goddess who is a military strategist and fierce fighter, just remember, it isn't about what women do, but the way we do it. Athena doesn't pursue fights for the purpose of domination. Rather, she fights to *defend* what is most precious to her. She is incredibly creative in her strategy, pre-ferring surprise and skill over shock and awe. Athena is less prone to lay waste to the town and more inclined to subtly slide into the town in such a way that the inhabitants eventually welcome her to the throne. Of course, she is lethal to those who threaten what she values, and she offers no mercy when her slaying ultimately allows life to thrive. When she needs to be, she is ruthless.

We can be the same.

In order for us to offer the life-giving waters from the oasis of our femininity to those we deem worthy, it is more than OK to be selective. In fact, that careful selection is what ensures that your most beloved people will always thrive in your presence! Limiting those who drain the well is beneficial not only for you but also for those you love. Please the people who matter most: the ones who cherish you and your well...being.

No More Excuses

Do you ever notice yourself apologizing? For yourself? For the actions of others?

It's time to stop.

This is a behavior we learn early on as little girls: to be sorry on our own behalf and excuse the actions of others, particularly the masculine. We may have seen our mothers excuse the bad behavior of our fathers, even explaining away harmful actions — sometimes claiming them as their own fault. We do it in the workplace, too. We see our masculine counterparts get away with offensive locker room talk, gaslighting, unfair career advantages, and we tell ourselves that it's our fault — we just need to chill out, believe them instead of ourselves, work harder.

If our emotions flare up and our expression of them catches someone off guard, we apologize for our feelings and repress them by calling upon logic to give them credence — as if they need to be proved to be believed. We learn of a partner's infidelity, and we excuse their transgression as the result of something *we* must have done wrong — *we* were too needy, or nagged too much, or somehow were not "enough."

Interestingly, this isn't something the masculine really does.

We rarely hear the masculine excusing their behavior, excusing transgressions, taking one for the team, or playing small in order to let others walk all over them.

But it's not a characteristic of the feminine, either — at least, not an inherent one. This is a culturally learned behavior. From the time we are small, we learn that most aspects of being female are shameful, less than, or undesirable. We learn to apologize for ourselves — and the behavior of others — as a survival mechanism, so as not to be cast aside. If we don't apologize, we may be seen as too aggressive, self-assured, cocky — we may seem too much like a man.

Take a recent example of an infidelity I learned about from a friend of mine. She has been with this man for a little over a year. They survived a bout of infidelity about six months into her relationship. She forgave him, and he promised never to do it again. The relationship seemed back on the right track, until she noticed him being secretive: playing on his phone at all hours, hiding text threads. Though her intuition nagged hard on her soul, she chose to overlook it and give him the benefit of the doubt, because he continually reassured her that everything was fine.

But her intuitive knowing did not relent, and one day she determined that she had to get at the truth. So she did the thing I think we have all done or wanted to do at some point.

She looked at his phone.

Lo and behold, long threads of intimate conversation with another woman confirmed her suspicions. When she confronted him that afternoon, his first response was not to apologize or assume accountability, but to express incredulity at the fact that *she had broken his trust* by looking on his phone.

Sometimes ethical boundaries must be crossed in pursuit of truth and the higher good. Nonetheless, she began apologizing. She conceded it was wrong for her to look at his phone and reveal his secrecy. She subjugated her own needs and her damning discovery by giving away her power and letting herself be in the wrong.

Reading this, I imagine you're as furious as I was — at this man for being unfaithful, for not owning up to his indiscretions, and for refusing to admit that the wrongdoing was his, *not hers.*

As I was consoling my friend, I kept hearing her habit of

second-guessing her intuition. "Well, maybe I shouldn't have looked," she'd say. "Maybe it would be better if I just didn't know."

Truth always sets us free.

It is our powerful intuitive knowing that urges us toward the truth. At all costs. For all reasons.

And this is never anything to apologize for.

It's time to make a pact: We need to stop apologizing for ourselves. And those around us. Period.

The only time it is acceptable to issue an apology is if we've actually done something that was not in alignment with our integrity. That's it.

Otherwise, let's be done with apologizing for the condition or movement of our body, the way that someone else perceives us, other people's actions, our history, our present, our future. Anything and everything.

Get "I'm sorry" out of your lexicon.

And for that matter, let's suspend *any* excuse making — particularly on behalf of others. One of the things that my friend did after she revealed her partner's infidelity was explain away his behavior: "But he had a difficult childhood! He's in a codependent relationship with his ex-wife! He has had some trouble at work lately!" If the agreement between the two of them was for an exclusive, monogamous relationship and he crossed that boundary, that is 100 percent on him. Not her.

Excusing bad behavior perpetuates bad behavior. If we are to be societal changemakers on behalf of the feminine, then it is *never* OK to excuse bad behavior. We cannot excuse the locker room talk of our colleagues, the inequalities on the playground, or the double standards in relationships. We cannot tolerate the procrastination on doing what is right or the rushing forward on the basis of decisions that don't benefit everyone involved.

And we certainly do not need to apologize for behavior that isn't even ours.

That goes for us, too. We can't make excuses for our smallness, our perceived emotionality, our devalued femininity. It's time to be *proud* of all of that, because it makes us who we are. It makes us women.

Ultimately, the more we *own* our feminine essence and all the qualities and behaviors that come with it, the closer we get to being a fully Satisfied Woman.

At Home with Yourself

It is time to come home to your feminine self. Let go of the tiredness, burnout, and constant litany of "shoulds" and return to your feminine nature. No one is served by staying too long in an uncomfortable and unappreciated state, whether that be in a relationship, a career, or even the state of motherhood (to the abandonment of any other identity). We as women serve the world when we return home to ourselves.

This returning home allows us to tend to the well of life-force energy within us. This is how the world thrives. Without our attending to this, it dries up and dies. So do we.

Satisfied sister, you know of what I speak. We have all been in situations where we have just stayed. Too. Long. This represents a gender-wide martyrdom, self-driven by the unappreciated value of the feminine. The feminine has been misunderstood as the *endless giver* of life energy, when in fact the feminine is the *receiver and cultivator* of life energy.

We must return to ourselves to fill up. To drink from that essential well in order to fortify ourselves for our continued creative journeys. We do not belong to anyone else — our spouses, our intimate partners, our families, or our children.

We belong to ourselves. We are sovereign. We have agency.

And because what we possess is so necessary to the world — so much so that they have contorted reality to make us believe *it is our duty to give ourselves away* — we must learn one of the most important words of the feminine domain: *no.*

I imagine shivers running down some of my readers' spines as I write this.

This is not a typo. I'm giving you permission — wait, I'm returning your agency and your right to say "No."

No may be the most powerful word we own as the feminine. And while this also may feel culturally counterintuitive, *it is right and good and powerful*. *No* allows us to remain at home in ourselves, to honor our energy, our intuition, and our internal feminine gifts. *No* enables us to regulate our nervous systems, prevent burnout, and apply our energy where it can best serve. *No* gives space to those around us to do for themselves while cherishing the unique life force that we possess. *No* returns any loose energy and attention back to us so that we can keep our own well filled.

No preserves our femininity. So that in the moments when we want to issue a clear, full-bodied *Yes!* we are ready, fortified, filled up with life energy.

Consider all the ways that you currently leak your life force by doing things that do not feed your feminine soul. Too many carpool trips to the kids' playdates and back. Too many shopping errands for the household. Too many uncompensated late nights at work. And while these may feel like basic responsibilities of adult life, ask yourself: *Are they? Or have we as women just been bamboozled into thinking that everything that is asked of us is our responsibility?*

It actually isn't.

In fact, we remove agency from others when we jump in to take care of everything and continue to be all things for all people all the time. Not to mention that we lose ourselves in the process. We overlook our own needs, we compromise on the Four Keys, we stuff down our intuition, and we mask our emotions. Continuously draining our well depletes us of our life energy, deadens our ability to experience pleasure, and ultimately diminishes our connections to others.

This kind of depletion leads to resentment. Resentment of our daily lives, the people in it, and those who seem unappreciative of our gifts. Resentment takes us out of our hearts and our feminine bodies and leaves us homeless, far away from ourselves. Resentment kills relationships and makes repair impossible.

In light of this, saying "No" is simply a smart life strategy! Pulling back your energetic output and protecting your feminine life force enables those around you to step up into the role of honoring your feminine needs and gifts. Whether it be your intimate partner, family, children, coworkers, or community members, their ability to contribute to *your* well-being and help you get *your* needs met creates radical accountability for everyone.

When we do everything for everyone, we let them off the hook. If we're constantly solving our teenager's problems, they never learn the resilience they'll need to handle their own business. If we always clean up after our intimate partner, they never learn to honor the space they live in and our place in it. If everyone around us gets used to us doing things for them, well, then, they never learn to do anything for themselves. And in this way the cycle continues, and our well continues to be drained.

We cannot be Satisfied Women if we have an empty well.

Making *no* a part of your lexicon empowers you to preserve your greatest resource: yourself. It reinforces your femininity and asks the world to cherish you and your needs. It allows you to drop the mask of masculinity and settle into the feminine power of receiving, which ultimately calls upon those around you to step up into *their* most empowered place.

No is not unkind. *No* is not selfish. *No* is one of the most important boundaries a feminine woman can set. And perhaps the most important boundary those around her can honor for her.

How do you know when to say "No"? Let your intuition guide you. Remember, your intuition is your greatest feminine gift. It directs you toward your greatest feminine expression. Anytime a choice is to be made, check in with your intuition and call forth a clear *yes* or a clear *no*. When a *no* arises, issue it forth like a golden seal on the moment and let the rest unfold unapologetically.

Consider the queen. Any queen, really. The queen isn't busy running around picking up groceries and doing laundry. The queen archetype embodies a principle of governance, guiding the palace and ensuring everyone around her is exercising their greatest gifts. Queens surround themselves with the most capable of people and *inspire* their loyalty and admiration. Queens are entirely at home with themselves, and in their home — their castle — they are the wellspring around which everyone who loves and cherishes them gathers.

Because society (and probably everyone around you!) is so used to women simply saying "Yes" to everything that is asked of them, your clear "No" may be met with resistance. This is not your problem to solve. Initially, this "No" may shock or destabilize those who receive it. But ultimately, as you continue to remain clear and steadfast in your boundaries, they learn to show you they cherish you, honor your energy, and do for themselves (or for you!) what you've requested. This allows you to settle more fully into your femininity and generates satisfaction in you — and, ultimately, in those around you, too.

The Perils of the Mask of the Masculine

While each of the polarities has its own qualities to be expressed in a balanced or distorted way, one phenomenon we see more and more often is the feminine woman who dons the mask of masculinity to steel herself for the world around her. Because we've been raised in a patriarchal culture, we learn to emphasize what is viewed as valuable (masculine qualities and pursuits) over what is deemed less valuable (feminine qualities and pursuits).

From the time we are little girls, we are told that we can be anything, we can do anything — and we'll have to compete with men to do it. Want to be an astronaut? You'll have to fight your way up a career ladder dominated by the rigors of manhood. Want to have financial success on your own? Sure you can, as long as you play by the rules and regulations set forth by men (rules and regulations that benefit them more than you). Want to live an independent life? Then you need to grow some balls, play by society's rules, and win on society's terms.

When it comes to finding intimate partnership, we are taught early that good men are scarce and that other women are the enemy in a competition to find the most desirable man. There is no "The more, the merrier"; rather, it's "May the best woman win." All this competition — against both sexes — following the rules of the game set by the patriarchy means that our standards are determined by the masculine, and we had better "man up" if we want to get along in today's world.

These perils and pitfalls of femininity mean that it is best tucked away and the hardened mask of masculinity donned. Now, for women whose primary polarity *is* masculine, this can prove much easier than for the feminine woman, though society may perceive her as needing to be "more feminine." Even so, she's probably well equipped and thriving in her masculinity in many ways.

But for the feminine woman, life in a man's world is hard. Hardening. Hardened. As we diminish the softness of the feminine within us and devalue or deny its qualities, we lose touch with that part of ourselves. It may not even be that we *forget* what it is like to be powerfully feminine; rather, it's that *we've never known what it was like to be powerfully feminine in the first place.* Because survival requires all of us to follow a preset masculine structure, leaning into the masculine is literally a coping mechanism for today's woman.

It doesn't work in the long run, though. While there are certainly times for any human to bring forth the masculine regardless of their natural polarity, the challenge arises when we are inauthentically stuck in that mode. This is an incredibly common occurrence today; we even see it in the most beloved and heralded women in our lives. Outwardly, it shows itself as all the qualities we expect from the masculine: leadership, strength, accomplishment, decision-making, logic, protection, and providership. Again, there are times in everyone's life when deploying these qualities proves to be the best course of action! It is when the feminine woman is fixed in this mode too long that issues arise.

In that case, those outward expressions devolve into behavioral patterns like control, bossiness, inability to see another's perspective, lack of intuition, suppression or second-guessing of emotions, entitlement, judgment, and possessiveness. While wearing the hardened mask of the masculine may help the otherwise feminine woman climb the corporate ladder and achieve the trappings of success as deemed by society, she is doing so from a deeply inauthentic place. That inauthenticity wears away on her as a profound regret and longing for her true self. When prolonged, it leads to overwhelm and burnout. Life feels exhausting because she receives no support for her feminine to relax and flourish.

This causes the suppressed feminine traits to come out in unexpected, uncontrolled ways. For example, emotions are a surprise and are unwanted for this woman; they certainly are unwelcome by intimate partners and other loved ones. The nagging feeling of an intuitive knowing she is ignoring is a source of unease rather than comfort. She feels resentment in her intimate partnership because her partner inevitably shifts to the feminine in response to her hardened masculine mask, and that is not what she actually needs. But she is caught in a trap: While she *desires* a strong masculine partner, he cannot show up in this way for her while she still holds tightly on to the masculine mask; but the idea of dropping it may be completely foreign to her. Or it may be terrifying because it means relinquishing control and surrendering to her true nature. When you've been raised to believe that femininity is both undesirable and dangerous, leaning into it feels tantamount to self-destruction.

It is easy to see the entrapment of this situation, particularly for little girls who enjoyed the opportunity to occupy the feminine prior to the onset of puberty. When small, we were raised to believe in Prince Charming and the idea of being saved by a courageous masculine. While the fairy tale is never true, the idea of the wholehearted masculine protecting and cherishing his beloved feminine *is* something we can aspire to! If this is alive in your feminine psyche, then moving through life with a hardened masculine mask eventually reveals a painful reality: we cannot permanently wear the mask of the masculine and hope to be cherished as the feminine by the people around us. The two cannot coexist.

And so the inauthentically masculinized woman faces a conundrum: to retain the mask and continue to sacrifice her feminine authentic self... or to drop it and create the space to thrive as the feminine and be cherished by the world.

Finding Your Allies

While the modern-day woman continues to face challenges from all sides in the pursuit of satisfaction, it is possible to find supportive allies on the journey. It may sound silly to delineate a list of feminine allies, but if you've never thought about it, it's time to take stock. We all need others we can rely on to help us grow, heal, and maintain ourselves as the Satisfied Woman. In general, we can seek out three main types of allies: friends, healers/mentors, and intimate partners.

For the purposes of building your team of allies, this list should include anyone who emotionally, energetically, and spiritually supports your efforts in embodying your feminine polarity to the greatest possible extent. These are the people who notice and tend to your well when it is drained, who fill you up and remind you of the power you possess. They are the few you invite to drink from your oasis, to share your energy — the few you trust to keep you in your center as a fully Satisfied Woman.

We all have people we adore wholeheartedly but who drain us; people with whom we have to be selective with our time and energy but still want in our lives. Cultivating your allies means making conscious choices about who serves what need for you, who is available to help you get those needs met, and — perhaps more importantly — what your needs are in the first place!

Friends

First on the list of allies are friends. The friends category can also include family members, but the emphasis is on the people whom we choose to be there for us, because family is complicated. Some family members we interact with out of obligation, and some we actively choose to have in our lives. Let our list of friend allies include all those we can count on, trust unconditionally, and feel nourished by when we are depleted, whether they are biological family or chosen family. Ideally, the family we love most are trusted friends, too, right?

Allied friends understand your mission and cherish your feminine nature while letting you be free to explore it. They affirm your primary polarity and also understand when life calls you to masculine up! You can count on these friends to remind you to release the mask of the masculine when the time comes, because they care about your emotional needs enough to see when you are drained. These friends have a close watch on your energy levels and are unafraid to call you out when you aren't leaning into your fullest feminine potential. They are there to support you and lift you up and keep you in alignment with your integrity.

Healers/Mentors

Your healers and mentors do the same. We all come into this life to be healed. The mere fact that we are human means we are imbued with complicated psychology. Add to that the fact that we are born women, and we definitely have things to tend to in the psyche! Because the unconscious, the domain of emotions and intuition, is the province of the feminine, spiritual and psychological exploration is essential for us as women. It helps us access our emotions, build trust in our intuition, and understand what makes us feel safe, secure, able to trust, and cherished (the Four Keys). Not to mention that the more integrated we are with our feminine energy, the more we are able to express it to the healthiest possible extent.

Healers offer many modalities these days, whether they be working on a physical, psychological, spiritual, or metaphysical level. If they have the tools to remedy what ails us, then add them to your list of allies. No longer do we need to pass up healing forms that seem stigmatized as "woo-woo" or "too girly." In this day and age, many forms of healing have become acceptable in the mainstream — and anyways, the urgency of our need to heal trumps any kind of side-eye we may get as a result. Try the singing bowls class you're curious about. Join the yoga studio that entices you. Book an appointment with the therapist your friend raves about. Sign up for the free acupuncture at your local school of Chinese medicine. Explore the tantra, Vedanta, Vodou, or Santería tradition your heart desires. If it calls to you, explore it. Find the women who practice it and let them bring you into the fold and initiate you into the healing they offer.

Along with healers come mentors. Mentors are those who have navigated a bit further down the path we are on and have something to offer us for our own journey. They don't need to be bona fide experts. They don't have to be designated gurus. They just need to be generous enough with their knowledge and insights to shepherd us along the way to our own satisfaction.

Intimate Partners

There will be times in our life when we are partnered and times when we aren't. We may have one partner for a lifetime or many partners throughout a lifetime. No matter the shape or texture of our intimate partnerships, when we have them, it's critical that they enhance our satisfaction and feminine well-being, that they allow us to thrive as women, and that they nourish us from the inside out. Our intimate partners need to be invested in helping us to grow. Our intimate partners must be those whose open hearts guide us more closely to the heart of who we are. They cherish our needs and prioritize helping us to get them met. And for whatever amount of time we choose to share a loving space with them, they have a positive impact on our lives, leaving us better off than when the relationship began.

These are the people we invite to our oasis. These are the people who help us to keep it filled and hold us to account, making sure we fill it ourselves, too. They are not drains on our energy, but fill us up when we are dry.

These people are precious. And yes, I know, these people may also be incredibly rare and hard to find.

If you don't have beloved friends and family: find them. If you have not started your healing journey: begin. If you're not currently inspired by a wise mentor: seek one out. And if love in intimate partnership is important to you right now, then leave your heart open for the right one.

They are out there.

Communion, Not Competition

While there is much to be said about the dynamic between the masculine and the feminine, there is also a lot to consider regarding the beneficial dynamics between feminine women. Unfortunately, in our culture female relationships are done dirty from the get-go. We are conditioned to please the masculine, to contort ourselves in the most impossible ways to try to "win"…win a partner, win in the workplace, win in academic settings, win in life. Perhaps worst of all, the "winning" requires us to compete with other women. We are pitted against our fellow females in ways that develop mistrust, fierce comparison, and judgment of both ourselves and them. As women, we are raised with an ethos of lack, made to believe that resources are scarce, everything must be fought for, overachieving is necessary, and being a "good girl" is the only way to get you what you desire.

We internalize the notion that we must have all the best stuff in a keeping-up-with-the-Joneses attitude, no matter how badly it breaks the bank. And this perception of limited resources isn't just about commodities: it extends to nearly everything. We need to maintain our looks to the nth degree, because appearances are everything and only the prettiest girls garner attention. The jobs we seek feature fierce competition, and not just with our fellow females — we must also be more accomplished and work far harder than men to get the same opportunities (but likely not the same pay). And don't forget the perception that finding the right intimate partner is a near impossibility, because the field is sparse, so we had better be the best, have the best, look the best, and only then may the best woman win.

It's exhausting.

At some point in our early lives we are imbued with these corrupted cultural values, and the competition begins. It wasn't always this way, though. Historically, women worked together for the betterment of one another and the tribe. Community and communion are powerful feminine values. They serve to uplift everyone we care about and ensure that no one feels left behind. The problem-solving strategy of the feminine is not about swift, solitary, and decisive decision-making, as it is for the masculine. Rather, the feminine is interested in a more egalitarian approach, including gathering a variety of thoughts and opinions on the matter at hand, then collaborating to come up with a solution that benefits the whole and gets everyone's needs met.

This kind of feminine companionship is beneficial to all. It doesn't compete, tear down, second-guess, or subjugate. It definitely doesn't backstab, gossip, or throw shade. To befriend the feminine again, we must first choose to befriend the feminine within ourselves. It is time to drop the repression of our intuition and the misgivings or shame we feel around our emotions. In this context, the most important thing we can do is release any tendencies toward comparison or jealousy. Comparison is a game that no one wins, because one person is always viewed as "more" and another as "less." Jealousy creates an imbalance of "mine" versus "not mine," where wanting something we don't have puts us in a state of lack. Comparison and jealousy automatically pit us against each other and make it impossible to be vulnerable in friendship. Joy and trust cannot exist in a hierarchical state.

And we need our feminine friends.

Our powerful skills of collaboration and communion with other women allow us to give voice to the uniquely feminine insights, intuitions, challenges, and changes that we all go through. Our ability to work together and support one another is grounded in our common experience, which validates what we feel, think, and know. Being a woman in the world is tough enough without our trusted feminine allies by our side. There is power in numbers, and if you wonder what kind of change groups of big-hearted, like-minded women can achieve, you only need to look to recent history with the nationwide knitting and donning of pink pussyhats to call out misogynistic behavior in politics and the development of movements like #MeToo that give space for women's stories to be believed.

We need to be believed.

On a personal level, it is gratifying and soul mending to have a beloved group of satisfied sisters with whom to share your stories. It is other women who offer the best advice, shoulders to cry on, and support in dealing with difficulties that we have not yet sorted out for ourselves. Yes, of course, there is also therapy. And intimate partnership. But even with those other outlets, there is nothing quite like having a close girlfriend (or a few!) to share heartache, excitement, agitation, and elation with. That level of feminine camaraderie keeps you knowing that you are not alone and helps you normalize whatever you are going through at the moment.

We need groups of women around us, whether that means one

good friend and ourself or a much bigger group of women aligned with similar intention. We need them to remind us of the power of our femininity and encourage our pursuit of satisfaction.

Everyone benefits from a woman's satisfaction. Including other women.

Rather than continuing to believe the patriarchal paradigm that competition is fierce, resources are scarce, and it's better to go it alone, we can shift into the feminine way knowing that there is always enough to go around and that friends and loved ones make all the difference in our experience of life.

Think of your grandmother. Or any elder matriarch in your life. The one who, when asked, always had an extra place at the table for a wayward friend or out-of-town family member. They didn't need to cook anything extra; they always had enough. Even if it meant everyone's plates were a little smaller, everyone's hearts grew a little bigger for the sharing of the merriment. This is the feminine way: inclusion, communion, creativity, and the nourishing of joy and pleasure.

We need to include our fellow feminine friends in the sharing of our satisfaction. As a culture, we hold sacred the "girls' night," but if you've ever watched a reality TV show, you know how they often end: with a so-called catfight and picking sides, or the women at each other's throats for throwing shade, or someone stealing someone else's intimate partner, or a supposed friend sneaking in underhanded judgments.

It's rough out there for female friends.

There is no need to make it so tough anymore. You can find other women out there desperate to connect on a soul level to their soul sisters, longing to bring forth the feminine in joy, safety, sacredness, and satisfaction. Find them. Love them. Share all you are with them. Remind them of the power of feminine connection. Understand that by sharing our resources with other women, we are actually feeding ourselves. We replenish our wells when we spend quality time with quality women. We teach each other how valuable we are when we reinforce the messages that we are all enough and that we are worthy of keeping those around us who feed our souls. We all become an oasis together.

Nourishing the Feminine

If women are the wells filled with life-giving and life-affirming energy, then we need to take seriously — perhaps even selfishly! — the need to keep ourselves overflowing with satisfaction. Our satisfaction means that our needs are being met and that our joy and pleasure are being shared with those around us. It's a win-win for everyone! And while we certainly need allies, friends, and loved ones around us who protect, support, and fill our well from the outside, we must also take responsibility for filling our wells from the inside.

The first thing to do is cast aside anything that drains you. Take stock of your daily life, your habits, and your guilty pleasures. I've always found that last particular designation ironic, because how could something that makes you feel guilty be pleasurable in the first place? It can't. In fact, a guilty pleasure is simply something that triggers a primal unconscious reaction that ultimately spirals into shame and negative thinking. Consider the way many use social media these days. Sure, they may initially log on to check in with a friend, but too many times that check-in devolves into doom scrolling and negative self-comparisons. Too frequently, we leave our social media time feeling bad about our lives, ourselves, and the use of our time. Not to mention that zero human interactions have ever benefited from the relatively recent practice of phubbing — ignoring your companion while paying attention to your phone. If a behavior ends in shame, guilt, sadness, or a sense of being sapped, it is time to remove it from your life with the kind of precision a scalpel offers.

Or the kind of efficiency that unstopping the drain in a tub offers. Let's be honest. Sometimes the well needs draining and clearing.

No harm in releasing stale energy that no longer serves us or things that muddy our precious feminine waters. To know whether something enhances your energy or not, notice how you feel when it's happening or when it's over. Things that enhance you make you feel more alive and connected to yourself. Things that drain you make you feel exhausted, burned out, and, well, drained.

Drained means you are disconnected from your femininity, or you may even feel as if you have armored yourself up to protect yourself. Drained means that not only is there not enough feminine energy to feed your soul, but you are sapped of any energy you may wish to make available to others. It's likely that you know the feeling of having to give more when you have nothing left to give — the very thought drains you further! It's a stressful scenario that puts us in a negative mindset and also has physical consequences: raised cortisol levels, lowered immune response, and all the other health outcomes that coincide with prolonged stress.

Being drained is not an option for the feminine anymore.

When you notice you're feeling drained, make a decision to remove that person, circumstance, habit, or thought pattern from your life. It may be your monthly book club that drains you. Quit. If it's the long commute that drains you, see if you can telecommute or alter your work schedule to drive at less stressful times. If the social media habit gets in the way of human interactions, consider cutting it out of your life altogether. And if the downward spiral of comparison affects your mood, lighten it up by consciously finding the good in others. Consider mitigating all the drains on your feminine energy. If it doesn't fill you up, you don't need it!

Understandably, not everything is removable...like that relative who always makes you feel like you need a nap after their visit or the tedious weekly meeting required by the job that you otherwise love. As the old saying goes, sometimes you've just got to eat your peas. But think of it this way: the things that are drains but nonnegotiable make it even more important for you to be overflowing — saturated — at all times.

What saturates our feminine energy? For lack of a less saucy but also less effective way to ask it: *What gets us wet?*

Our feminine energy is nourished by creativity, pleasure, sexual and sensual fulfillment, opportunities to receive what is generously given by others, and communion with the feminine, either within ourselves or with others. And remember that it is not *what* a woman does, but *how* she does it. Women find creativity in painting as well as in construction. We find pleasure in tending to the garden and also tinkering with machines. We find sensual and sexual fulfillment in solo endeavors and in partnership. We love receiving whatever is generously given, whether it be a massage or a new power tool. Communing with the feminine can mean a fun day out with the girls or doing the spiritual and psychological work of delving into the feminine aspects of the psyche.

Whatever society has told you about what girls should want or what women can do, forget about it. Use the directive of keeping yourself overflowing — *wet* — to explore what most excites, enlivens, and enthuses you. When it tickles your feminine fancy, no matter what it is, know you have hit gold. When you feel alive inside, when you feel that wellspring full to bursting, you know you have stumbled on something or someone who needs to stay in your life. Join the women's motorcycle group. Find the knitting circle you have heard about at work. Relearn the skill your dad shared with you as a kid that you used to love. Engage in the form of therapy that makes you feel most free. Feminine is a *feeling*, and anything can bring it on as long as it makes you feel most connected to yourself — as long as you feel the satisfaction in it!

8

Redefining Success as Satisfaction

Satisfaction is not an end goal. It does not have parameters or produce statistics. Satisfaction does not have a ladder to climb or inherent competition to beat. Satisfaction involves no sweat, toil, effort, or overachieving. Satisfaction also never sells itself short.

Satisfaction is a feeling. It is the pleasure — the complete joy and delight — we feel when our needs and wishes are fulfilled. Whether those needs and wishes are met through our own efforts or through support from others doesn't matter. We receive the pleasure either way. Satisfaction may be solitary or collaborative, but let's be honest, satisfaction is better when shared. Who wants to be satisfied alone?

We may experience quiet moments of joy when satisfaction creeps up from within us. But for the big wishes and needs we fulfill in life, we know that pleasure is enhanced when we are surrounded by friends, loved ones, and family who share in the experience.

Satisfaction is the way of the modern feminine woman. And it is time to revise long-held assumptions.

The societal idea of success, with its goal-oriented milestones, inherent competition, and measurable wins, is not the way of the Satisfied Woman. The rules of success were not written by us.

The way of the Satisfied Woman is being written by us. Now.

We determine our satisfaction. We decide what wishes and needs are most important to us. And the way we fulfill them? Well, that's up to us, too.

It's time to ask yourself: *What is it that truly makes me satisfied in life?* Forget the conventional notions of success or following previously scripted models of how life "should" look. What makes you the most satisfied? From what do you derive the most joy? The most pleasure? What fuels your creative spark?

I recently discussed the premise of this book in a conversation with a group of incredibly successful women — movie industry professionals in Los Angeles. When I revealed the title and the overall gist of what I was writing, their faces lit up. They responded with comments like these:

"I've always hated going to board meetings. It just never felt right."

"I always wished I could just collaborate with people to find solutions."

"As soon as I got my promotion, I realized it wasn't what I wanted."

"I wish I could just relax a little and not worry so much about what other people think."

When I defined *satisfaction* for them, they became giddy and wondered why they hadn't considered that satisfaction is so preferable over success. They chimed in about how much they enjoy working *with* other women rather than against them. They were excited by the idea that they didn't actually *need* to do it all or be it all for everyone in their life. You could hear sighs of relief and feel tension fall away from their shoulders. The amount of struggle and stress the feminine has held throughout these long patriarchal centuries is unfathomable.

We don't need to carry that anymore.

It was never truly our burden to bear. And it never suited us to begin with.

If the core element of satisfaction is fulfilling your wishes and needs, then it is essential to know what your wishes and needs are! As I've said before, we have no need for metrics, deliverables, or keeping up with the Joneses. We simply want to define the wishes and needs that, when fulfilled, give us the greatest feeling of pleasure. There is not one scripted list of wishes or needs that result in satisfaction!

If you wish to earn a degree, then fulfill that wish.

If you need to feel safety by being surrounded by friends and family, then fulfill that need.

Some women wish to start their own family, while others don't need to have children of their own. Some women pursue traditional success in their career, while other women wish to spend time outside of a traditional career path. Defining your own wishes and needs is critical, because otherwise you cannot know what it will take to fulfill them.

Let's consider fulfillment. To fulfill something is to bring it to completion or make it a reality. Again, here we leave behind concepts of competition, winning at all costs, or striving for some pinnacle of achievement that you may never reach. Instead, fulfillment suggests a sense of manifestation. I'm not talking about law of attraction woo-woo or wishing something from nothing. Instead, fulfillment is the manifestation of your greatest needs and wishes *through action.*

The other powerful thing about satisfaction is that it does not need to be DIY. Success, especially as we define and value it in modern culture, is a solo pathway; satisfaction often comes through joint effort. Success is hierarchical, relying on an elevated social status as perceived by others; satisfaction is not. Success comes at any cost; satisfaction offers dividends. Success is exclusive, while satisfaction is inclusive. The way of the powerful feminine always focuses on inclusion and collaboration. The feminine understands the benefit of sharing rewards.

When I was about thirteen years old, my mother was the tenth caller on a radio show sweepstakes. She won a thousand dollars. For a single mother working at a community center and living from paycheck to paycheck, this was a huge deal. Neither of us had ever seen that much money at once in our entire lives. In addition to paying bills and buying groceries, my mother offered me a hundred dollars of her winnings to do with what I pleased. This was my first lesson in feminine collaboration and sharing.

When the feminine has what it needs, it joyously shares the rest. When her well is full, she offers the life-giving waters to those she loves. When the feminine is satisfied, the people around her also thrive. It's what fuels our pleasure centers. This is why satisfaction is our aim as we reclaim our feminine power.

Making Your Wishes (and Needs) Come True

As we've covered in this book, the essential needs of the feminine lie in the Four Keys: safety, security, and the ability to trust and be cherished. Those are the needs of the feminine as a whole, but how you define and achieve them is up to you. What you need in order to feel safe and secure, how you establish trust in relationships, and the way you desire to be cherished — each of these is as uniquely individual as the snowflakes that fall from the sky.

Think of the Four Keys as a matrix over which to lay your own needs and wishes. Needs are nonnegotiable: for example, we need a roof over our head, or we need a relationship to be monogamous. Wishes are achievable: we wish that the roof over our head be in a certain location or have so many bedrooms, or we wish for our intimate partner to love true crime stories and date nights as much as we do. The fulfillment of both needs and wishes is essential for satisfaction, for the feminine to be able to experience joy and pleasure. Without needs met and wishes fulfilled, life becomes stressful and unenjoyable.

Don't sacrifice your wishes for your needs. Don't sacrifice your needs for your wishes.

Imagine these two things as the pillars — the foundations — for your satisfaction. We cannot erect the roof of satisfaction without both needs and wishes being tended to. Never compromise your needs. Never give up on your wishes.

And don't overlook the inherent feminine quality of collaboration in getting them fulfilled! In fact, consider building yourself an alliance of people who contribute to your satisfaction. As I've said, the feminine path is not solitary, and cultivating the right helpers for the journey is a skill. These are the people you invite to gather at your oasis, drink from your well, and share in your joy, pleasure, and satisfaction. They are your allies, your loved ones, your beloved(s), and your most sacred sisters and friends.

While members of your alliance may come and go, what they must all share with you are your values. Or at least they must understand and uphold your values in order to buy into your needs and wishes. If their values are not in alignment with yours, it proves very difficult to find motivation for the journey. Consider an apathetic employee who cares little about the company's bottom line. Or a bored teenager's lackluster investment in a clean room. If their values are not aligned, the person isn't a good fit for your alliance.

Your values are what you build your life around, what you believe are your essential qualities, or what drives your biggest decisions and dreams. If, let's say, people you love were to describe your top three qualities, what would they name? If you were to make a list of three nonnegotiable qualities in your life, what would you write down? Would you include integrity? Honesty? Family? Loyalty? Nearly any quality can be a value, so long as it is important to you.

Of course, they say it's a woman's prerogative to change her mind, so you might even find that your values shift throughout your life! Perhaps when you are in the sensation phase of your early twenties you value education, fun, and friends. Then, as you evolve into the integration phase in your forties, you value integrity, adventure, and exploration. There isn't a list that is for women only. There are no rules. You can value whatever you want, so long as it helps you honor your intuitive emotions and express your femininity fully. While we may have many values, identifying your top three values in life can help make big decisions *much easier*. Knowing what you value is…invaluable! It helps you clarify who you are and what you are about, and it guides your ability to make decisions that solidify the foundation of the Four Keys in your life.

Understanding your values is also a crucial component in developing relationships. You may already have been a part of a workforce that had established team values. Perhaps you were hired because your career goals seemed to be in alignment with the values of the company. This is a pretty commonplace thing for businesses these days, and it is also important for any other relationship you hold dear. Defining the values of your family or your intimate partnership, for example, offers a structure for how to make decisions and reach common goals within that relationship.

I have had the great pleasure to officiate the weddings of quite a few friends in years past. It's not a mere matter of standing in front of their wedding parties and helping them recite vows! On the contrary, an officiant's job is to counsel the couple through the entire process of union, ensuring that they are in alignment on all the elements of that ritual. One of the most important tasks I assign my wedding couples, well before the wedding date, is an exploration of and commitment to core values as a couple. While each individual has their own values (again, I recommend a personal top three), and there is likely some crossover in those values with an intimate partner, they are not always the same. The assignment often inspires a lot of discussion (sometimes heated) to determine the couple's four main shared values. Four values between two people gives them a perfectly square rubric in which to work, a balanced structure that invites even sharing and contribution.

The point of having shared values in intimate partnership is to create a structure for the relationship that is outside of your individual selves. In this highly individualized day and age, we tend to get caught up in the "What about me?" question. But in a truly symbiotic partnership (which is where the feminine most thrives), the values of the couple offer something greater than ourselves to serve and uphold. That kind of selflessness by each individual demonstrates to the other that the relationship is the highest priority.

When decisions come down to a question of "Will the outcome serve *my* needs or the *relationship's* needs?," a truly balanced intimate partnership demands that the relationship take precedence over the individual. True love *costs something.* It requires a little bit of sacrifice. That's what makes it precious, worth fighting for, and even worth dying for. The human heart is built to love, and we are hardwired for this type of connection. The word *compassion* comes from the Latin roots that mean "passion with," and *passion* originally meant "pain." So to have compassion for another is to hold a little pain for them inside your heart, to know that you gave just a little of yourself over to their greatest good.

Because that's what intimate partnership is: making sure that all our decisions serve the highest needs and wishes of the relationship. Even outside of intimate partnership, an alignment of values is what ultimately gets needs met, too. Friendships, family relationships, and work partnerships all benefit from aligned values. It is what allows people to collaborate to fulfill their goals and ideals. It is what changes our world, our communities, and our individual lives. When we work toward a common good, we achieve great things.

As part of the feminine ideal of collaboration, we work with others around us who share our same values, and together we make good decisions on how to proceed. While the masculine in these endeavors likely makes decisions from a place of logic and reason, the feminine (who can also employ logic!) likes to ultimately base decisions on intuition and feeling. This is how the feminine establishes clear boundaries.

Boundaries are what keep people safe. They are necessary and helpful as we collaborate with others to make our wishes and needs come true.

Understanding what a boundary is is simple: It is just a clear yes or a clear no. It doesn't require logic or reason, but it does need to be expressed. If we don't express a clear yes or no when we feel it, then it's likely our boundaries will be crossed. A breach of boundaries is a faltering of the Four Keys. Anytime we have a breach of boundaries, it degrades our sense of safety, security, and trust in the other, and we do not feel cherished. When this happens, we become unmoored and must work to correct the course.

Understand, too, that there is a difference between an unvoiced boundary and a boundary that is willfully breached. An unvoiced boundary may be a result of shyness or fear. A willfully breached boundary is an act of aggression. Either way, the feminine suffers. Any opportunity we have to voice, establish, and uphold a boundary enhances the safety, security, trust, and well-being of all involved. It promotes goodwill and keeps positive momentum going.

It is with this positive momentum and trust in those around us that we successfully fulfill our greatest needs and wishes. In turn, we are able to help others do the same. For the world of the Satisfied Woman is not selfish — it is selfless. Boundless. Limitless. When our cup is full, then that cup runneth over. When our oasis is nourished, we share that life energy with others.

Let's Talk about Success, Baby

In a recent conversation with one of the most powerful women in my life about the difference between success on a man's terms and satisfaction on a woman's terms, she came to a stunning epiphany. As I explained the power of femininity and how it differs from masculinity, she realized she had made a critical and all-too-common error as a woman. Having risen to the top of the publishing world with a C-suite position, she was recognized as one of the leading professionals in her field. She had spent decades chasing what she was taught were the ideals of success.

She confided in me that even though she was certainly proud of her accomplishments, *she wasn't satisfied*. I explained to her that it was likely because we have been taught to achieve success on a man's terms.

As a popular saying goes, "There's nothing worse than climbing to the top of your ladder only to realize it's on the wrong wall."

As women, we often build our ladders on walls constructed by men. It is *their* version of success we are groomed to chase after. They have created the rules by which we are all supposed to play, and they define the cutthroat nature of pursuing a career. Our culture tells us that we are capable of doing anything…at all costs. We are fed these ideals from an early age.

While there is nothing wrong with pursuing a career and achieving career goals, perhaps there is a different way to do it and be satisfied.

What if we, as women, pursued career *satisfaction* instead of *success*? What would that look like?

Instead of dominating the boardroom, we establish a round-table of discussion to collaborate on ideas and get everyone's needs met. Instead of deliverables, we focus on achievables. Instead of emphasizing profit margins and bottom lines, we emphasize employee happiness, satisfaction, and growth.

Inspiringly, women already do this.

Companies owned by women are more integrative, family-centric, and collaborative. Female business heads concentrate on communication and collaboration and utilize their intuition to drive business decisions. Female entrepreneurs tend to keep businesses smaller and more manageable in order to nurture the happiness and well-being of their employees. When women earn more, typically, they reinvest those earnings back into the business and the people who work for them. Women are more relationship centered than task centered in the workplace, and they tend to focus more on personal goals than on overall business goals.

Women are in business to be fulfilled.

I learned this the hard way when my own solopreneur venture suddenly had an explosion of success. Nearly overnight my business grew tenfold, and I had a much bigger business on my hands than I had ever anticipated. From the outside, it looked like a raging victory.

But on the inside, I was miserable. I was drowning in spreadsheets and expansion plans. My workforce grew beyond what I could personally manage. I was losing touch with the elements of my business that were most important to me, and because the day-to-day running of the business overtook my focus, I was no longer able to tap into my creativity.

Boy, was I successful in the traditional sense. And I was stressed beyond belief, tasked with making decisions that were not just outside of my comfort zone but outside of my integrity zone. I learned that at that level of so-called success, the relationships I'd built and the values I'd established for my business were difficult to maintain. I tried desperately to hold the reins of this beast and continue to drive it into greater and greater profitability.

But at some point, I had the realization: I was not happy.

I pulled things back. Consolidated my efforts. I stopped focusing on the numbers and shrank my business to a more manageable size, one that allowed me to maintain my relationships and my creativity. I stopped chasing male-defined success (which in my case was unfettered business growth) and instead started moving toward satisfaction.

While, statistically speaking, women-owned businesses traditionally make less than their male-owned counterparts, I have to wonder: Does that translate to less happiness? It didn't for me.

Knowing what we do about the financial disparities of women in business, I'm not advocating that the differential should not be overcome. Women need to be able to make all the money their hearts desire — and *also* consider how much their heart's desire is to truly be happy and fulfilled.

Satisfaction comes from the fulfillment of our dreams. When we dream of a fulfilling career, it includes not just financial prosperity but also the things that the feminine values so highly: continued creativity, collaboration, sound relationships, and happiness through the work. If we're not happy with our career or in our workplace, no amount of financial success will make that right inside our soul.

Earn as much money as satisfies you and create as much good in the world as you can through your career. At the end of the day, let it fulfill you from the inside out.

The Problem of Money

Part of the problem of the patriarchy is the notion that money is to be earned mainly by men. In our culture, there is an almost inseparable coupling of masculinity and moneymaking. Men do generally find purpose through their career and the ability to materially provide for their intimate partner and family. The masculine thrives when he has a true north to guide him forward, and that sense of direction is often inspired by his responsibilities to career and family. But while earning power does coincide with the essential masculine qualities of providership and purpose, it is not the only bar by which to measure masculinity. There are many ways to provide for the family, especially in today's more diversified environment. And purpose may be found in avenues other than a traditional career path.

The problem we as women face is: money. If earning money is so conflated with masculinity, what do we do as feminine women? How can we shift that perspective so that we not only earn all the coin we can but also remain in our feminine nature while doing so?

This "money as masculinity" issue raises several challenges. First, the culture has taken this notion to an extreme with the inherent financial disparities that face women, who still only make eighty cents on the dollar compared to men. Second, the masculine-dominated workplace, where money is typically earned, makes it difficult for the feminine woman who doesn't play by masculine rules. Third, the feminine woman who earns her cash and brings home more than her masculine man frequently has a problem, because even though it means the couple can pay the bills, her higher earning power often translates to a destabilization of polarities.

These are not easy challenges to solve. Money is fundamental to our ability to live, be safe, and provide for ourselves and those we love.

Interestingly, it is common for women to either shy away from money, pretend as if they don't make it, fear asking for more of it, or feel shame for loving to have it.

Fact: having money is awesome.

While the saying goes that money can't buy happiness, that is actually not true. Statistics show that happiness is more easily achieved when individuals earn what they need to cover their bills and also have enough to enjoy their life and invest in their future. In the United States, at the time of this writing, that translates to around seventy-five to a hundred thousand dollars per year, depending on what area of the country you live in. Beyond that number, more money does not actually translate to more happiness. But it does afford you the ability to do more with your life.

No matter how much money you earn or even how much money you want to earn, hope to earn, or will earn in your future, you absolutely deserve to earn all that you can and never be ashamed to earn what you need *or to ask for more.* Money is a reality of life.

When women have it, they share the wealth. It's something they use to invest in others, too.

Let's give women all the money!

Money itself is not masculine. The earning of it doesn't need to be exclusively masculine, either.

We have a cultural issue of the masculinity of the workplace, but that doesn't mean women have no options to earn money on a woman's terms. When women employ their creativity, collaboration, and intuition, it is more than possible to create wild financial success. We don't have to work and earn solely on a man's terms anymore. When we bring our feminine strengths to bear in our career, that can translate into earning power!

Many of us learn this the hard way, because the historical pathway is the way of the masculine. After years of fighting that uphill battle of success at all costs, a lot of women realize they have climbed the wrong hill. But there is a different way. Plenty of women are employing their feminine gifts as a means to financial fulfillment. There are greater options than ever before for women to begin their own businesses, based on their wishes and needs. There are more women-owned businesses that embrace the values important to the feminine. And it is possible to bring your own values into the right career setting in order to help shift the culture and thrive.

It's time to earn on a woman's terms. Earning cash as a woman feeds our creativity; it fills our well; it offers us the safety and security we need to take care of ourselves and our loved ones. Money is as nourishing to the feminine as it is to the masculine. Given the coupling of money and masculinity in our culture, though, many masculine men have difficulty when it is their feminine partner who brings home the bacon. Even good-hearted men who love their fiercely powerful women run into this challenge when it feels like the providership is not in their hands.

One couple that I know finds this to be their main source of unhappiness. She is a freelance CEO who works from home and calls her own shots. He is a law enforcement officer — a perfect role for an inherently masculine man! Law enforcement is not a high-paying career, however, despite its inherent risks, so the wife is the primary breadwinner in this marriage. It doesn't take long at a lunch with friends before this issue comes up. At the heart of it is the masculine polarity *and who wields it.* The wife believes that due to her earning power, she deserves more decision-making clout for the family. For her, higher earnings equate to more control. The husband believes that this is a partnership, the money earned is *theirs*, and her earning capacity should not equate to more control, which makes him feel emasculated.

It is easy to see that the money issue creates both a power differential and an imbalance of polarities. Remember the Key Question I mentioned in chapter 6? When I ask this couple the Key Question, the wife emphatically responds with a desire to be cherished, while the husband is clear on his need for respect. Regardless of paychecks, the polarities thrive when they have their needs met, and the relationship thrives when decisions are made for the mutual benefit of both members.

How does the feminine handle finances? Let's look to Lakshmi, the goddess of abundance from the Hindu pantheon, for inspiration in this matter. She is depicted seated on a flowering lotus (the sacred flower of India, representing divine knowledge), with an endless stream of coins dripping from her four hands. There is no sense of lack or longing for Lakshmi. She is a confident woman who knows, unequivocally, that she has all the abundance she needs.

I'll share with you a story about this goddess. Lakshmi is invited to stay in the home of an Indian family through their devotion to her. Their daily rituals, or pujas, demonstrate their adoration for her gifts of abundance and prosperity, and over several generations, the family wealth and good fortune grow.

Eventually, Lakshmi comes to the father to say she must leave and spread her blessings elsewhere, but before she goes, he can ask her for one more boon.

After consulting the family, he decides to ask Lakshmi for the gift of peace of mind, so that they always know they have what they need, they are provided for, and they lack nothing. She delights in their clever request! Because this is her essential nature, she says, she is now obliged to remain in that household.

For the feminine, wealth equates to abundance, riches equal prosperity. Knowing that nothing is lacking is peace of mind. Financial success is not about the amount of money in the bank but about the prosperity and peace of mind it offers to you and those you love. Abundance is an attitude as much as it is a bottom line. It is less about how much we earn and more about how generous we feel when we spend it.

I remember a story from one of my teachers, who talked about her grandma during the Great Depression. She would throw open her cupboards and shout to the household how full they were! Of course, they were bare as bones. Regardless, her mindset allowed her to utilize what she did possess to uplift herself and her family and still offer nourishment and a sense of prosperity even through difficult times.

Lakshmi embodies the feminine free-flowing generosity that is actually the *knowledge* of inherent prosperity. Let that be awash over your household. Let the riches you have — in whatever form they take and however they are earned — represent a peace of mind that brings you and yours great fulfillment.

A Note about Financial Disparity

I am keenly aware that many women are financially disadvantaged or have little to no control over their financial situation. I write this book in the fervent hope that these disparities are changing and that our culture is waking up to the value and power of women. Women deserve financial equity, prosperity, and abundance in all its forms, as well as the independence to decide how to earn their money and what to do with it. As this book sits on the shelves and works its way through the culture of readers, my hope is that our world and its attitudes toward women and money change for the better. May there be financial freedom for all women.

It's OK to Not Do It All

Let me be clear. Women *can* do everything. We prove this time and time again when we venture into spaces once solely occupied by men. In any arena they choose to enter, women are capable of thriving, innovating, and excelling. In looking at cultures and careers once dominated by men, we now find more and more examples of women gaining their footing and finding success in all fields.

The playing field is still not level, however. We still have much work to do in this regard. Equity has not yet been reached.

While the feminine rights movements have strived mainly for equality, there is a lot to be said for *equity* being the better goal. Equality gives everyone exactly the same support and resources, whereas equity adjusts support and resources on the basis of need and capability. Generations of patriarchy and suppression have left women with a heavier burden to bear in terms of carving out their own life and career. It's like facing a giant mountain and being asked to climb it, except that every woman starts with a fifty-pound boulder strapped to her back that no man has to carry. Equality says that is fine because everyone is at the same starting line facing the same challenge. Equity gives her what she needs to get to the top in a fair way.

It doesn't make her less strong, less capable, or less determined. It means that she needs a head start, an extra push, or a flatter road to reach the summit. Until that fifty-pound boulder is removed (when our culture and society resolve patriarchy), we need to be sensitive to the needs of women and all disadvantaged populations and support their efforts and desires.

We also need to be sensitive to our strengths, values, and desires as feminine women. Because while women can do anything they set their minds to, and while women are capable of succeeding at any task, men and women simply have different strengths and values.

These differences themselves are not the problem. It is when the differing strengths and values are seen as a weakness or a detriment that the problem arises. That's when we can achieve neither equity nor equality.

By honoring the differences between men and women, masculine and feminine, we allow each to thrive and find fulfillment on their own terms. While the fight for equality has been and continues to be fierce, and losing ground in that battle is in no one's interest, it is important to recognize that the strengths inherent in our femininity mean we excel in certain areas that those on the masculine polarity may not. There are some fields that we are more suited to, some differences that actually make us stronger and more valuable! The feminine polarity gives us heightened access to our intuition and emotions. The unique way that girls play throughout childhood gives us practice and understanding in social interaction and emotional regulation. And, as we've seen, the feminine energy thrives on creativity, collaboration, and connection.

If these qualities are at the heart of who we are, why would we *not* lean into them and use them to our advantage in our life and career? Why wouldn't we play to our strengths and kick ass and take names while occupying a role that deeply fulfills us?

Sometimes the current cultural narrative — the one that has us vying for equality on masculine terms — makes women feel as if we need to be more logical, tough, rational, task oriented, and regimented. We actually don't need to be any of those things if it is not intrinsic to our nature. Of course, we are each unique, and the varying degrees to which the masculine and feminine manifest in us give us all an individual mix of strengths to harness. However, for those of us in whom the feminine and its qualities are deeply rooted and fully realized, there is no longer a need to apologize for that, to try to be something else, to toughen up to match society's demands, or to retrofit ourselves into a masculine role if it is not in our nature.

It is A-OK to be a woman in this world.

Whatever role most suits you, whatever strengths you most want to employ, to whatever degree the feminine (or masculine!) manifests in you, play it to the best of your ability. Stop worrying about whether or not you can or whether or not you should. Rather, lean into the feminine intuition that is ingrained in you and follow your heart to pursue your dreams and achieve your fulfillment.

The Power of Sisterhood

We all love a fun girls' night. It's a cultural phenomenon replete with reality shows that highlight it, outfits that complement it, and happy hours that honor it. Whether your favorite girls' night activities include staying in or going out, being with a multitude of friends or a handful, if you've ever enjoyed the pleasure of dedicated time with your favorite group of females, then you know what I mean when I say: "Boys, keep out."

For generations, women have been kept out of men's spaces. Whether it be exclusive men's clubs or societies, or activities and outings, our society has long featured places that only men occupy. For the most part, they can have them (barring the places that would *benefit* from inclusion). These opportunities for men to commune with one another are essential — and the way they nourish the healthy masculine benefits the feminine as well. The masculine is energized through unstructured time (think of their fishing outings or camping trips) and time with other men in their exclusive circles. They need their boys' nights, their time together to recharge and reset so they can be centered in their healthy masculine expression.

We need that, too, for the feminine.

We need the bonding and camaraderie of sisterhood to reconnect with the feminine. Though it tends to look very different than that of our masculine counterparts, we also need our ladies-only time to recharge and recenter ourselves. Our bonding time generally includes a lot of conversation and emotional support. We toss around ideas and collaborate on solutions. We explore creative ways to refresh our mindset and emotional well-being. We support one another's struggles because we inherently know what it is like to be a woman in the world.

And we can't do all this effectively with a man present.

Even one penis in the room changes the environment. The focus becomes less about nourishing the feminine and more about tending to the masculine, because of our cultural conditioning. While men may feel left out of women's spaces or sacred girls' nights, a little separation is OK. (It is not OK when it becomes pure segregation or ostracization.) Our time together as women reinforces our best qualities and allows us to work through challenges with the support of our sisterhood, whose intuitive insights cannot be matched by the masculine. And our ability to stretch our emotional wings in this way is essential for the other parts of our life.

Basically, time with our fellow females is good for the other people in our life. When we bond with other women, that energizes the feminine energy within us. It reconnects us to our intuition, validates our emotional experiences, and helps us draw conclusions through the collaborative input of our friends. It also reminds us of the value of other women, and takes us back into our deep history when tribal women spent time together regularly solving the problems of one another and the tribe as a whole. It was through healthy discussion and sharing of ideas that the workings of the tribe were refined, conflicts resolved, and innovation advanced to better the well-being and functioning of all.

Shit got done.

This is a refreshing reminder of what happens when collective groups of women collaborate. Especially in the face of the patriarchic cultural notions designed to separate us. Modern-day women have been taught to compete with one another and that resources are thin. "May the best (wo)man win" is the doctrine of the masculine — when, in fact, sisterhood and collaboration are at the heart of feminine power, and coming together to collaborate is where our creativity has the potential to most effectively change the world around us. It is in this feminine space where we value fulfillment over achievement and satisfaction over success.

Women need sacred spaces. Whether they are in person or virtual, whether they are built on lasting friendships or on temporary business relationships, whether they include women of different ages, backgrounds, ethnicities, environments, or beliefs, women need places to come together and collaborate. This is where we find out who we are, what we stand for, what fulfills us, and how we want to change the world around us to enhance our satisfaction.

There is much to change. Let's get it done.

9

Ascending the Throne as the Satisfied Woman

Look up the term *queen*, and you find two incredible definitions. The first refers to the woman who is the ruler of an *independent* state. The second definition describes the most valuable piece on the chessboard — the one that moves wherever she damn well pleases.

These definitions perfectly encapsulate the conditions of the Satisfied Woman.

Let me update our working understanding of the word *independent*, as well as the word *state*. *Independent* does not mean alone, isolated, or in a vacuum. As we've learned throughout this book, the feminine exists — and excels — in collaboration and relationship. She needs allies, friends, intimate partners, colleagues, family, and others who help her get her wishes and needs met in order to give rise to her fullest expression. *Independent* in this context also does not mean the woman who does everything for herself, exists in isolation, and dons the mask of the masculine to her detriment while hardening to the feminine beauty that is her nature. No woman needs that kind of *independent*.

The independence of the queen is *inward dependence*. She relies

202 The Way of the Satisfied Woman

always on her greatest gifts, her feminine, intuitive, emotional knowing; and she knows her inner truth so unashamedly that it guides her every decision. A queen never falters in that *inward dependence*. And a queen's decisions are never questioned, most importantly by herself. A queen who second-guesses herself is no queen at all; she has lost the independence of her own state. In this condition, this queen cannot move where she pleases, for she is bound by the constraints and rules of the patriarchal world around her.

When a queen is the true ruler of an independent state, that state is her own body. Her own agency. Her own psyche. Her own intuition. Her own emotions. And she rules that sovereign realm with grace and aplomb. The independence has nothing to do with the outward masculine world that values a DIY culture and then asks women to do more. The true queen's independence is of her own making, based on the confidence she cultivates in her intuitive, emotional knowing.

As the ruler of her own independent state, the queen calls her own shots. She determines who and what she surrounds herself with. Think of *Alice in Wonderland*'s Red Queen, who continually shouts, "Off with their heads!" While no literal beheadings may take place in our sovereign state, the metaphorical beheading is the removal of anyone who tries to force their way into our world without honoring who sits on the throne.

That throne is ours.

It is time to get comfortable. Like the great Egyptian goddess queen Isis, the queen in us knows the throne as a place of repose, of serenity, of ease. When we are on our throne, our world delights and supports us. Our needs are met, our wishes are fulfilled. We are satisfied. And we are served by those around us who honor our gifts and adore what we bring to the queendom. They gather around the oasis we have cultivated through our creativity, collaboration, and excellent decisions that benefit all. Our comfort is their comfort. Our well-being fosters theirs. Our prosperity results in their abundance. It is a queendom for the benefit of all in our world.

While we seek harmony, grace, and comfort — and do what we can to cultivate these qualities — things do not always go smoothly. As the queen, we understand there is always change. There is always upheaval. Queen Elizabeth II, the longest-reigning monarch in British history, lived through seven decades of great transformation, and through it all, she inspired the devotion and cherishing of her nation. I was fortunate to be at a lunch table with a dozen British airline pilots on the day of her death. Upon the announcement of her passing, one stood up, raised a glass, and said, "The queen is dead. Long live the king!" The sadness in the air was palpable as they mourned their beloved feminine monarch. They had all been inspired by her for their entire lives, and some had even served her in earnest as members of the Royal Air Force.

Inspiring the cherishing and devotion of those around you is not an easy task for a queen. It takes incredible connection to your femininity, great faith in your intuition, and a commitment to keeping an open heart. Think of the iconic Queen of Hearts in any card deck. She is perhaps the most beloved of all the cards, a symbol of love and devotion. To receive a Queen of Hearts card is a cherished thing, something that signifies your status in the heart and life of another. I have been the very fortunate recipient of many Queen of Hearts cards, given to me by my beloved masculine partner. He found the first one at a sexy circus event in Brooklyn and magicked it from my hair as we were dancing. The tradition was born, and over the years, he has presented them to me in the most surprising of ways in all the important moments of our life together. I have received Queen of Hearts cards in foreign countries, in castles, on boats, at dinners with friends, and in quiet moments between just the two of us. I honestly don't know where he gets so many of this specific card or how he finds ways to deliver them that still surprise me. I am now surrounded by dozens of Queen of Hearts cards in my home as a continual reminder of his devotion to and love for me, his feminine partner.

I do not recount this story for any reason other than to share how incredibly important and empowering the love of another is in the life of a woman. It has changed my life. All women need to have someone who delivers the proverbial Queen of Hearts card in surprising moments to remind her just how cherished she is and how grateful the giver is for her feminine gifts and the oasis of life energy she offers. Whether that person is an intimate partner, a beloved friend, a loving family member, or a member of the community who recognizes her benevolent sovereignty over her world, such an act of cherishing shows us that who we are, the love we give, and the gifts we share are honored in the world. It reminds us that through the fullest expression of our femininity, not only are we healed and elevated, but we heal and uplift those around us as well.

Through all the challenges that we may face as the queen of our own independent state, we must remember that none may be overcome if we disconnect from our femininity, forget our intuition, or harden our heart to the world around us. That kind of queen rules with fear and destruction, and the world has no more place for that type of governance.

What the world needs is the healthiest expression of femininity possible for us to muster. And even though the world itself throws many obstacles in the path of the feminine, it is a worthy endeavor to overcome what we can and reveal our feminine gifts. For too long, we have suffered in the old patriarchal model. And while both the masculine and the feminine suffer under patriarchal distortions, it is always the feminine, with our keen intuition and fierce inquisitiveness, that raises the alarm and sounds the call to make things right. Queens are the ones who inspire great change. It is for the love of a queen that a Royal Air Force or other military branch goes to battle. Like the great goddesses Athena and Diana, the feminine does not shy away from doing what is necessary to benefit the greater good.

For us, the battles may take place in our home or our workplace. They may take place in the bedroom or the boardroom.

Wherever they take place, let them be on *a woman's terms*. Fueled by our intuitive guidance and innate knowing of what feels good and right and true for all. Women fight for the well-being of those they love. These are the fights worth fighting. This is energy worth exerting.

When we stand in our power — no, when we sit on our thrones — we inspire change in the world. It starts with the open, loving, receptive heart of the queen, who knows intrinsically what allows the members of her queendom to be happy and thrive. The queen knows what satisfies her and what satisfies all around her.

As we settle into the comfort of our own throne and don the crown of our sovereignty, let us rule over the world we find ourselves in with the foremost qualities of the feminine. Let us be fully realized as feminine women and endeavor to create a life we are completely satisfied with.

Finding Your Way as the Satisfied Woman

The path to queendom is not a given. Unlike the seats of power of many official regents, our throne is unfortunately not bequeathed to us at birth. It must be won through the intuitive action and open heart of our life journey as we wade through the perils of an outdated patriarchal culture. Thankfully, there is a way for women to realize satisfaction.

Throughout this book, we have taken a look at the challenges women face in our culture, the pitfalls we must overcome, and the various ways to differentiate our feminine path from that of the masculine. The path of the feminine woman is different from that of her masculine counterparts. It is not less than, *it is hers*. Ours. It is replete with the things that matter most to women, and it is grounded in our strengths and values.

In a world that is finally starting to realize the incredible power of women and the benefit of ensuring our equity and equality, we must start following the way of the Satisfied Woman in order to demonstrate for other women around us and those who will come after us that satisfaction is possible on a woman's terms.

Our journey in this book has allowed us to explore all the facets of life affecting the feminine and the ways we overcome and reconcile our unique challenges in order to fulfill our wishes and needs. From the cultural condition, to the way we were raised, to the unique aspects of a woman's body and psyche, we learned myriad ways to address what represses us and bring forth our feminine to the greatest extent possible. To bring this process into focus efficiently, here are the highlights of what we learned about the way to satisfaction:

- **Know what satisfaction is.** Satisfaction is the pleasure derived from the fulfillment of your wishes and needs. It is what most feeds the feminine and allows us to express ourselves fully.
- **Ask the Key Question.** In intimate partnership, do you want to be respected? Or do you want to be cherished? The first answer that arises reveals your natural polarity. Those who want to be respected are primarily in the masculine. Those who want to be cherished are primarily in the feminine. Knowing your polarity is critical to navigating your own life and relationships.
- **Establish the Four Keys as your foundation.** These are essential for the feminine to flourish. They are safety, security, trust, and the ability to be cherished. Make sure that your life and all the people in it help you keep the Four Keys in place. Losing any one of them is destabilizing and disconnecting for the feminine and prevents you from experiencing joy and pleasure.
- **Revere your feminine gifts.** There are many feminine gifts. Primary among them are your intuition and your capacity to feel emotions fully. When you receive

intuitive guidance, heed it. When you feel emotions, allow yourself to experience them. Surround yourself with people who honor and cherish your emotions and believe your intuition.

- **Take your time.** A feminine woman's life is governed by time. Her biological clock is real and dictates when it is the right time for her to do anything: embark on a career, explore a relationship, pursue parenthood, change direction...you name it. A primary question of the feminine is "When?" Honor your phases of life and the periods of time that matter to you.
- **Heal thyself.** Explore the feminine domain of the unconscious in order to resolve all that is holding you back from fully expressing your femininity in the healthiest way possible.
- **Always get your needs met.** There is no overstating this point. Happy people have their needs met, and as you know if you've read this far, a key definition of satisfaction is the fulfillment of wishes and needs. Fulfill your own needs and never overlook the opportunity to receive help from others to get them fulfilled, too!
- **Never give yourself away.** Women no longer need to be all things to all people at all times. When you feel drained, honor yourself by releasing what drains you or limiting contact with it.
- **Maintain a full well.** Prioritize what nourishes and reenergizes your femininity. Whether it is via an activity, time alone in a quiet space, or communion with friends, keeping your well filled helps you maintain your connection to yourself and allows you to access your creativity, pleasure, and joy.
- **Seek satisfaction, not success.** Success is a masculine paradigm in the form of an end goal that may not even bring a sense of completion or happiness. Satisfaction,

however, is a feminine model that allows you to fulfill your wishes and needs through immersion into what brings you the most pleasure.

- **Get comfortable as queen.** As you settle into your throne as the Satisfied Woman, govern your independent state (that's you!) with grace, an open heart, and discernment. Surround yourself with those who feed your soul and fulfill your wishes and needs. Be exacting about removing everything that detracts from your satisfaction. When you are satisfied, so are the ones who share your world with you.

As women, we do not need to walk a linear pathway to the finish line. Rather, our way is circuitous, winding, and always subject to change. As you consider the elements that contribute to your own satisfaction, feel free to tackle what is most pressing for you first. It is possible that you are fully satisfied in some areas of life but not others. Try to focus on what is possible for you right now, what you can update, upgrade, exchange, or excise in order to take steps — baby or big — toward your personal satisfaction. As you do so — as you fill your well, remove what drains you, and prepare your throne — every improvement will yield dividends for your well-being as well as that of those around you.

Remember, the way of the feminine woman is not solitary. Ours was never meant to be a solo journey. The people who surround us matter. Make sure they are the most supportive people for you. Let go of the fear of firing your friends, your family, or anyone who doesn't serve your highest good. Because if they can't serve yours, then ultimately you can't serve theirs, either. The feminine is as ruthless as it is careful. It is always looking to preserve and energize life anywhere it can, which sometimes means releasing or quashing what snuffs it out. Focus on what enhances and enthuses your femininity and watch how the fruits of that particular labor also fulfill the people you care about.

It is an important journey. Not just for you as a feminine woman, but also for all those women who look to you for friendship, support, and inspiration. We are in this together. We always have been! The way of the Satisfied Woman becomes easier to traverse as more women choose to walk its path. The more we tamp down the weeds and remove the rocks blocking the way, the more well-worn the path becomes, so that women who follow us have an easier time finding their way to fulfillment. As you walk the way of the Satisfied Woman, you make it easier for other women to do the same.

Blessings of the Queen

As we become fully satisfied, we females become more fearless. Time and life experience show us our inherent power. If we stand firmly in our satisfaction and in our own femininity, then this is when we are, in fact, the most beautiful to behold.

When we have the wise years of experience behind us, when we have taken ourselves back from whomever we have inadvertently given ourselves away to, when we have fulfilled the satisfaction of our wishes on our own terms, when we have raised our family or community (whether chosen or biological) and passed the torch, then we are fortified with the kind of experience written into the ancestral psyches of our common experience…and we pass that wisdom down to future generations of women.

As we ascend onto the throne of the queen, we discover ways to maximize our impact on the world and lean into the womanhood we've survived in order to pave the road for those who will come after us. This is our responsibility as women, especially in a world changing as rapidly as the one we live in today. How do we want to affect that change? What values do we want to instill in the young women who look to us for guidance? And how can we gracefully retain our sense of pleasure and connection within our intimate partnerships in order to continue to be supported and receptive throughout life?

A question that begs to be answered by all humans is this: *What is my legacy in this life?* All humans wish to be remembered beyond the years of their mortal life. We live only for as long as the last person who remembers us. A sobering thought. What do we want to be remembered for? How do we want to be remembered? What people value most at the end of their life is not what they have accomplished, but how authentically they lived and how hard they loved. As women, we understand that to be satisfied — to fulfill our wishes and needs — is the greatest mark of a life well lived. It doesn't matter what is in our bank account or how many deliverables we made. No one cares about how many days we called in sick or the times that we struggled to meet a deadline.

What matters, and what you can account for *now*, is your level of authenticity as a feminine woman and toward the people around you whose lives you touched with your feminine heart. Authenticity and openheartedness are traits appreciated by all humans, regardless of polarity. But when the feminine woman steps into her most authentic, vibrant self, it means we are living in the most powerful way we can: by the intuitive guidance of our soul. While it is simple, understandably, it is not easy. This is how we move mountains. This is how we unfailingly do what serves the highest good for us and those around us. This is how we inspire other women in our life to do the same.

This is how we *live* the way of the Satisfied Woman.

Acknowledgments

This book has been stirring inside me for quite some time. Recently, that stir became a roar as I felt a shift compelling me to bring it to life. I have felt the responsibility and gravitas of this work and am deeply honored to offer it to the world.

Of course, this has not been a solo endeavor. None of this would be possible without the graceful support of so many in my life — too many to name. However, there are some who truly have given me wings and allowed *The Way of the Satisfied Woman* to take flight.

First and foremost, I must name my grandmother, Maria Barlowsky. I was told once that we only live as long as the last person who remembers us, and when I heard that, I vowed that my grandmother's name and her incredible legacy would never be forgotten as long as I live. Her lessons to me as a child echo in my heart decades later, and her suffering and hardships continually inspire me to honor her by living my life with as much compassion and joy as possible.

Many other women in my life have given their unending support to this work, including my mother, Pola Taylor, who fostered my fierce independence from day one as a child and has never stopped being my most ardent cheerleader.

My dear friends Danél Lombard, Margie Woods, and Emma Segal and my stepmother, Nancy Bush, all generously offered their feminine perspective and incredible scholarship in reading initial drafts of this book. These women inspire me daily and made this book richer through their personal history and inquisitive feedback.

I would not be in the fortunate position of bringing this book to life without the literary team who tirelessly and graciously threw their weight behind me and believed in this book from the start — namely, my literary agent, Michele Martin, and Georgia Hughes, editorial director at New World Library. These two incredible professionals have boldly paved the way for other women in the field and made it just a little easier to have our voices heard. Both Michele and Georgia championed every word and offered me the most exquisite mentorship and guidance throughout the process.

It is an honor and privilege to once again be working with the team at New World Library to bring this book to life, and they have not missed the importance of this work in helping to polish it and ensure its impact. I thank my deft editor, Diana Rico, who wields the cleverness of the goddess for whom she is named. Additional gratitude goes to Kristen Cashman, managing editor; Tracy Cunningham for art direction and the beautiful cover design; Tona Pearce Myers, production director; Monique Muhlenkamp, publicity director; and Tanya Fox, proofreader.

The feminine is duly empowered by the protection and support of the cherishing masculine, and I could not be more grateful to have my beloved partner, Gareth Bird, by my side through this endeavor. It was his love that gave me the confidence to pitch this book at the start, and his constant strength that the waves of my own discourse broke against as I worked through the emotional process of writing this book.

To all the women in my life who have been present for this

process, supporting me in the decades that led up to it, and to those who will continue to do so in the years to come, I write this book for you. May this work inspire the feminine to find its foothold in this complicated modern world, and may each of you women find your unique path to the greatest satisfaction possible.

Notes

Chapter 1: Redefining Femininity for the Satisfied Woman

p. 17 *"The pussy is the portal"*: Traver Boehm, *Man UNcivilized* (self-pub., 2019), 208–9.

Chapter 3: Permission to Disrupt

p. 47 *"the womb and the tomb"*: Joseph Campbell, *The Hero with a Thousand Faces* (1949; repr., Princeton, NJ: Princeton University Press, 2004), 105.

Chapter 4: Making Meaning on Our Own Terms

p. 67 *Joseph Campbell's famous question*: *The Hero's Journey: The World of Joseph Campbell*, dir. Janelle Balnicke and David Kennard (1987; Silver Spring, MD: Acorn Media, 2012), DVD, 58 min.

Chapter 5: Healing the Feminine Psyche

p. 119 *"turn her into the man"*: *Yellowstone*, season 1, episode 7, writ. and dir. Taylor Sheridan (Los Angeles: Paramount Network, 2018).

p. 123 *"HAPPINESS ONLY REAL"*: *Into the Wild*, writ. and dir. Sean Penn (Los Angeles: Paramount Vantage, 2007).

Chapter 6: The Satisfied Relationship

p. 144   *"When people show you"*: Maya Angelou quoted by Oprah Winfrey, "When People Show You Who They Are, Believe Them," *Oprah's Lifeclass*, Oct. 26, 2011, https://www.oprah.com/oprahs-lifeclass/when -people-show-you-who-they-are-believe-them-video.

About the Author

A lanna Kaivalya, PhD, is an author, educator, speaker, and thought leader in the field of women's empowerment and femininity. She has written five books, developed international training programs, and taught audiences around the world. She earned a doctoral degree in mythological studies and depth psychology from Pacifica Graduate Institute and spent more than twenty years studying psychology, the human condition, the nature of the feminine and femininity, and Eastern spirituality. Her education has given her a unique perspective on femininity, and her work centers on equipping women with a better understanding of what it means to be a woman in the modern world. Her day-to-day efforts are focused on offering empowering resources through her website, including *The Satisfied Woman* podcast, her blog, and her exclusive women's community and online courses. She lives in Los Angeles and finds great satisfaction in sailing to Catalina Island and riding horses. Find out more and connect with her at TheSatisfiedWoman.com.